THE ROCK BAND HAND-BOOK

THE ROCK BAND HAND-BOOK

EVERYTHING YOU

NEED TO KNOW TO GET

A BAND TOGETHER AND

TAKE IT ON THE ROAD

Words and Illustrations by Kathryn Lineberger

A Perigee Book

A Perigee Book
Published by The Berkley Publishing Group
200 Madison Avenue
New York, NY 10016

Book design by Richard Oriolo
Cover design by Joe Lanni
Cover illustration by Joe Lanni

First edition: October 1996

Published simultaneously in Canada.

The Putnam Berkley World Wide Web site address is
http://www.berkley.com/berkley

Library of Congress Cataloging-in-Publication Data

Lineberger, Kathryn.
    The rock band handbook :   everything you need to know to get
a band together and take it on the road / Kathryn Lineberger.—1st ed.
        p.   cm.
    "A Perigee book."
    Includes index.
    ISBN 0-399-52237-9
    1. Rock music—Vocational guidance. 2. Rock music—Economics
aspects. I. Title.
ML3795.L475   1996
781.66'023—dc20   96-11444
                                                             CIP
                                                             MN

Printed in the United States of America

10   9   8   7   6   5   4   3   2   1

$\mathcal{C}$ONTENTS

Contents

CONTRIBUTORS

Every one of the nice folks who helped me put this book together deserves a lot more than this lame little mention, but unfortunately words are about all I can spare. My appreciation is vastly understated below.

Generous **Melissa Allen** provided Rolodex access, sweet **Ritchie Baxt** fixed everything, **Christina Bradley** thought it seemed like a good idea, **Loren Chodosh** bought lunch and assumed a jurisprudent demeanor for just long enough, **Kim Colletta** & Jawbox loved their fans that much, **Chris Cush** appreciated the needs of the financially challenged, **Robin Danar** explained sound so well, ever-optimistic **Pati deVries** let me cry on her desk, stylish **Anita Diamant** rocked, **Lee D'Onofrio** organized his thoughts, **Jonathan Feinberg** spent fifteen years to become the best drummer I spoke to, **Antony Fine** threw a party on the Fender Rhodes, the fabulous Miss **Laura Galpin** sparkled and shined, **Mary Gormley** knew it when she saw it, **Susan Henderson** provided the pie, **Brian Kelly** wanted everyone's music to be good, my best friend **Anna Kim** learned it all with me and suffered by my side, other **Linebergers (Martha, Mary, Sara)** just got love, **Lotion** too, **Pete Min** maintained a kickass collection, **Joe McGinty** remembered, **Claire R. (Relentless) Pasta** started the whole thing, **Irene C. Prokop** made it so much better, **Perry Serpa** had a lot of good ideas up his sleeve, **Kurt Ralske** imparted what he learned the hard way about creative temperament, **Jim Rondinelli** gave it up in the car, **Tim Thomas** uncensored himself, **Rose Thompson** knew more than she realized, fiercest-ever **Janet Treadaway** also learned it all with me except that she knew more to begin with, turn-on **Craig Wedren** (and **Shudder to Think**) did put out, **Lisa White** achieved club booker sainthood, **x-Fluffer** members inspired me, and **Tony Zajkowski** had to go very last because this list is alphabetical.

THE ROCK BAND HAND-BOOK

HEY, COOL THING

(Introduction)

My **best friend** had an idea. She skated into the restaurant where I was eating dinner with some friends who play in a pretty successful band. "If these guys can do it," she asked with certain logic, "why can't we?" I had never given musical expression a single thought in my life. "We could be like those groups who just play two notes and scream," she reasoned. The members of the pretty successful band raised their eyebrows and smirked. That convinced me.

"OK, I get bass." I figured that since it had only four strings it would be easy to play. That weekend we met a girl with primary-red hair who played oboe in high school and wanted to learn drums. An ex-roommate wanted to sing, and John's girlfriend said she'd learn guitar. Cool! We would be lounging on leather furniture signing record contracts in no time!

Well . . . none of us knew how to play any instrument (except oboe), so we sat around in each other's living rooms eating tortilla chips, listening to tapes, and trying to figure out who might lend us instruments. Within a few days we had collected a sorry array of equipment: we had an acoustic guitar, a New Wave–looking bass, and some phone books and a flea market "native" thing for the drummer to bang on. After a few weeks we had learned the proposed two notes and played them in a v e r y s l o w arrangement which we called a song—it sounded not one bit like any decent band I've ever heard. The leather furniture would have to wait, but surely (chuckle) we would be onstage at CBGB playing our first show in a couple of weeks. Even if we sucked.

During the three years that followed, the band evolved a lot. A snare drum and practice pads replaced the phone book, and the little red five-piece drum kit that came next was replaced by a sparkling new wine-colored Pearl kit. Evangeline took over the screaming duties for Beth, then Krissy, then Vanessa, then Laura. Anna stepped in after Isa with a borrowed Flying V knockoff, which was returned in favor of a new SG. A generously loaned Les Paul replaced Connie's also-borrowed acoustic, and then Janet replaced Connie and bought a used SG to take the place of her Musicmaster. Two years later, only me and the tortilla chips have survived to tell the stories of those first living-room endeavors. And we did suck when we played CBGB.

My band started with nothing—no instruments, no members, no knowledge—and became one of the most popular bands in the neighborhood. I learned everything I know by doing it the wrong way at first or by watching someone else do it better. I asked stupid questions, I embarrassed myself, I made mistakes, and I played more than one show out of tune. As it turned out, my ignorance was a good thing. If I had known then what I know now, I would have looked at the prospect of starting a band and seen a foolish, unrewarding project that would plague my life. But I didn't know any better. The whole thing seemed like fun back then: hang out, eat food, play bass, kill time. I had jealously watched my friends in the pretty successful band (now I know why they thought this was all so funny) form, record two albums, and tour this country and others. Not only does my lack of knowledge make for some amusing retrospective stories (we didn't play at CBGB for another year and a half), but it got me to this point.

Too bad I didn't have a helpful little manual like this one—the kind that other do-it-yourselfers have—to guide my every foolish step. If I had wanted to add a mud room to my house or attend law school or open a 7-Eleven, plenty of resources would have been available to guide me—cable TV shows, seminars in Holiday Inn conference rooms, and of course entire aisles in bookstores. No one has written a book on how to be in a band—why not? (Even the movie *This Is Spinal Tap* offers more insight than anything in the library.) Often you read an article in some music magazine that marvels at some artist's self-taught genius. Why the awestruck reaction? How else does one learn to play, by majoring in pop songwriting in college? (Actually, you could, but I won't get into that.) What should really amaze the interviewer is that the gifted prodigy managed to get people to play in a band with her and listen to her music.

I wish my band had had a reference book written by someone with years of experience. Maybe then we wouldn't have so much gray hair today. This book is my wish come true, a bit late, but now you get to read it. As I wrote it, I referred to my memories of the bad old days, asked many more stupid questions, and picked lots of dead brains to come up with as much information as possible. In New York City's East Village, where I live, more rehearsal spaces, music stores, record shops, nightclubs, and recording studios thrive than in any other neighborhood (except maybe Nashville or L.A.). Many of my disenfranchised neighbors, as well as other musicians across the country, had stories to tell and advice to offer.

I hope this book will prevent the problems I had from happening to you; give you inspiration to continue when things get rough (things will get *very* rough); and let you know what to expect every step of the way. With the book as your tutor, you can enter the realms of trouble and shame vicariously by reading about them, then return to reality, unscathed but all the wiser. You should concentrate on making good music that you will love hearing and playing, and leave the horrible details in experienced hands.

Each chapter will teach you one important band function. Some parts are pretty technical, others deal with the psychology (ahem!) of the creative mind, and others have many stories, but none of it will challenge you too much. A rating of the subject matter's pros and cons will introduce each chapter and give you a preview of the activities, with notes about what you need, what kind of attitude adjustments you can expect to make, and how dirty you'll get. Musical integrity is often the least of your worries.

Before we get into it, take a glimpse at the possible glamour that awaits you as a local musical fixture.

Imagine yourself at 4:30 A.M., on a Saturday morning one year from now. Normal folks have had their Friday night fun, they dressed up and went out on dates, and now they doze in comfy beds. Not you, you're in a band! After leaving work early to run home and change clothes, you and your bandmates dragged 250 pounds of rock 'n' roll trappings up (or down) several flights of stairs and tossed them into the back of a shabby, borrowed van.

Onward from there, you fought rush-hour traffic to get to a show three hours away at the edge of a neighboring state. You arrived too late to get a sound check but in plenty of time for a slice of the world's most foul pizza. The usual crowd of college students that this club attracts has deserted—oops, it's spring break. Approximately eleven people showed up, probably by accident, and your lame performance scared them down to half that. Secondary cigarette smoke damaged your lungs while Marshall stacks ruined your ears; you collected your $25 (pizza money!) and loaded up the van. On the way home the faithful optimist in the band counted all the things that could have gone wrong while the diehard pessimist pointed out those that did. Someone cried. At least they kept you awake enough to drive.

So now you have run aground in the dead of the morning on filthy concrete steps, trying to drag 250 pounds of crap back down (or up) the stairs.

Can you deal? But don't fret, because fleeting moments of rock glory prevail. Imagine another scene.

Your band takes a booth at The Egg and I, after rehearsal, to discuss the details of shared pennilessness and have a grilled cheese. Two guys walk up. One looks like Beck but has done something stupid to his hair. The other is deliciously freckled and cute.

"Hey, um, are you guys Necrofilet?" asks the Beck-alike nervously.

"Yeah! (Unfortunately—hehe)," you answer. The two cuties look at one another, kind of nodding and acting nervous.

"Cool," says the talkative one, edging away from the table.

"Bye," says the other, continuing to nod.

I swear that making music will be really fun; and you'll get much more out of the experience than just learning to stand onstage and play eight songs at some tiny bar. As this book trains you to play in a band, the band will prepare you for life's greater challenges. Boot camp, marriage, religious cult deprogramming, hazing, espionage, running for public office, or talking your way out of a hostage situation ("Just put the gun down, and we'll play the intro any way you want, won't we, guys?") could all be part of your future with the skills you develop in your band. Unfortunately, adding *Drummer and Oboe Player for The Nubile Parade* to your résumé might not impress those potential employers like it should. But do you *really* want to work for someone who has no sense of humor?

1

WANNA BE IN OUR BAND?

(Getting Started)

NECESSARY MATERIALS: None.

ATTITUDE: Let's party.

FILTH FACTOR: Very low, 1½ out of 10.

DANGEROUSNESS: Fear not the unknown.

OPPORTUNITIES FOR ROMANCE: A few, but bandmates make bad dates.

MUSICAL IMPORTANCE: Not nearly as high as social importance.

PRICE: Free.

TIME: With speed dial, ½–3 hours; without speed dial, 1–2 days.

POTENTIAL FOR HUMILIATION: No, no, this is supposed to be *fun*.

ands begin easily. You can probably think the whole thing through with friends during a ten-minute ride to Dairy Queen. Smooth out the details over a Peanut Buster Parfait: decide who will play which instruments, what you'll call yourselves, what your music will sound like, and how you will accept your MTV Music Award. You really don't need much to get started. Every one of the musicians on every single one of your records started the same humble way, they learned an instrument, formed a band, and played shows. Seriously. Kim Gordon may be cooler than you now, but she didn't always play the bass and Sonic Youth would not exist if she hadn't decided to pick it up and try.

A Brazier may bring you closer to reality; you begin to ponder the qualifications, commitments, and logistical details. The name you chose five minutes ago now sounds dorky. Do not give these little obstacles another thought. Allow me to demonstrate how your three biggest fears will work in your favor. You do not have as much to overcome as you may think.

BIG FEAR NUMBER 1: "WON'T A LACK OF MUSICAL SKILLS HINDER MY EARLY PROGRESS?"

Don't be silly! Observe this fascinating rock paradox: you can make music without being a musician; you can remain ignorant of note names, chords, and standard rhythms; and you can even become a truly kick-ass guitar player (or bassist or drummer) without ever formally learning these skills. History has shown that this is so. Certainly, playing your instrument with skill and precision is a beautiful thing, and Chapter 2 will put you on the road to proficiency, but greater bands than yours have gotten onstage with less training.

Technical ignorance gives you a certain creative advantage, too. Skill-free, you will put together songs based on which fingerings are easiest and which rhythms you can manage. Players who know what they're doing often spend most of their time trying to achieve a specific sound. They eliminate musical quirks and mistakes that don't fit into their idea about what comprises a proper song; but these quirks bring your music a special quality, and they'll make your music totally original.

BIG FEAR NUMBER 2: "I'M BROKE!"

Broke is good, because money just doesn't fit into the picture. (Notice how even the successful artists behave as if they lack funds.) If you somehow do have a bank account, get ready to close it out—

you're headed for destitute territory. Musical equipment is expensive, but that ain't the half of it. Transportation, rehearsal space, recording, etc. all cost big bucks; and if you worked a normal job during the time you spent doing band stuff, you'd have that much extra cash. Just try not to think about this too much or, as one musician told me, "you'll start drinking."

Pauperism bonds you with other musicians in a way that even music can't. Just like a bunch of geriatrics kvetching about their gall bladders, any bunch of musicians loves to swap financial woes. Evictions, calls to parents for cash, constant borrowing (be careful about this one), and other dismal events will ensure the purity of your experiences, and give you some social basis.

To complete the picture of the tainting dollar's evil influence, watch how other musicians treat a band with finances that they did not earn making music. ("Look, mommy and daddy bought Steve a new amp for Christmas. . . . Let's kick his ass!") Their equipment is all new—no electrical tape holding it together, no technical difficulties—they came to the gig in a plush new van, and even their clothes are new. Shallow, yes, but no one respects a rich starving artist, so embrace your poverty—for now.

BIG FEAR NUMBER 3:

"BUT . . . I'M A SUBURBAN GEEK!"

And successful musicians are not?! Please take a closer look at your idols and imagine them in the eighth grade—J Mascis, Tori Amos, ooh, and Michael Stipe! Come, now. And those are just the artists. A legion of grown-up geeks work their nerdy little fingers to the bone making the music you listen to, including producers (dweebs), engineers (dorks), bookers (weirdos), and even (ahem) journalists. They certainly didn't grow up in tour vans surrounded by indie rock trendsetters. You'll fit right in.

A suburban upbringing, especially a really sucky, boring one, uniquely qualifies you to rock out. How many fanzine interviews do you read where an artist says, "I loved high school so much—class president and all—that I cried on graduation day," or "I started my first band with the rest of my cheerleading squad," or how about "Alienated? No way, man, I had tons of friends." The suburbs may seem like one of life's atrocities, encroaching from all sides. Ignore. The music you love was made by suburban kids who grew up and decided not to take the obvious path.

Maybe you're not ready to thank your parents for choosing to rear you in America's lovely heartland; but you can turn your torturers—crisply manicured lawns, a counter job at Bagel Nook, clueless guidance counselors—into song lyrics.

Since the music is already close enough to your life that you can submerge yourself, nothing really stands in your way if you want to participate. Rock 'n' roll isn't some science that you need a Ph.D. to practice. Just wanting to qualifies you, so jump right in.

Get Something to Play. First, find some instrument to play; try for a guitar. Anything that makes noise will serve your beginner's purposes, but a guitar probably makes more rock sounds and helps write more rock songs than any other thing you could play. Besides, guitars are much easier to come by than pianos or trumpets or whatever. Pause for a moment to reflect on your favorite guitarless bands . . . you see my point. Tooled up with a guitar, you can do it the Liz Phair way or take the Joan Jett route or follow P. J. Harvey's footsteps. A lot of music sounds great without guitar, but you need to learn the basics, and guitar is one of them. Until you can afford that sampling software or learn how to play something else, start they way everyone else did. Acoustic or electric, it doesn't matter what kind or how crappy, just so long as it has strings. With this choice item, nothing limits your rock options.

Words from Two Experts

Tim plays guitar and sings. He says if you're just starting to play and want to buy a guitar, GO ACOUSTIC. "Electric guitars make too much noise for you to hear what you're playing, they're too rock 'n' roll. The acoustic is more personal and great to learn chords on. Once you know them on an acoustic, which has a pretty challenging neck, you'll play them with ease on any electric."

Anna Kim plays guitar. She disagrees. "The cool thing about learning on an electric guitar is that your music sounds like real badass rock and if that's the kind of guitar player you want to be, then it's encouraging to be able to make loud noises right away. Besides, you can always unplug the thing."

Find Some Bandmates. Next, you need people to help make music. Since you do this thing to have fun, seek those whose company you enjoy, like the guys you drove to Dairy Queen with. Before you ask the potential rockers if they seriously want to do it and will congregate on a regular basis to play music, remember that you can easily find friends who want to host *120 Minutes* or lip synch in front of a camera, but it takes a little bit more than whimsical forecast to write a song. Could you marry these people? Could you spend 48 hours together in a small room recording songs, or two weeks in a grubby van (betcha can't wait) touring the South? Deep abiding love you don't need, but if you do like them and think you can create together, they'll do for now. Besides, they're already hanging around all the time.

Maybe you hold your friendships too dear to risk them in a band relationship, maybe your friends busy themselves with honor society activities and have no time to form the next Buzzcocks, and you've been writing songs alone. Even lacking human resources, you can start by yourself and the band will eventually form around you. Practice your singing, learn a little guitar, and spread the word that you want to play. They'll show up.

Formulate a Lineup. After you decide who is in and who is out, you must figure out together what each of the players will contribute. The conventional rock band has two guitars, a bass, and drums—so what? Only wedding bands need adhere to that configuration. (Go for it if you look good in a tuxedo and want the big bucks.) For the rest of you artists, play what you feel like playing and keep an open mind about the way it looks or sounds. There are no rules about what comprises an acceptable lineup but some people might not want to play in a band whose members include a violinist or lack a bass player. If such an attitude plagues your progress, just remind the conformist that many interesting, listenable songs come from unusual lineups.

Solo: Bands with a single member are quite rare, but some musicians do labor under the belief that if you want something done right, do it yourself; and through the magic of multitrack recording techniques, they can play all the instruments on their recordings. When it comes time to play a live show, however, such Machiavellians gotta hire people or beg musician friends to learn the music and get onstage. Wait until you sprout a hefty ego to go solo.

Two-piece: Depending upon the type of music you want to play, two bodies may be enough to make all the sounds. More than likely, you will still be begging other musicians to join you onstage.

Three-piece: This pretty common setup usually means drummer, bass player/singer, and guitarist/singer—like in Nirvana, for example. But other configurations are also possible.

Four-piece: Sometimes the four piece works like an expanded three-piece, with a singer who does not play, or plays another type of instrument, like violin or accordion. The Doors had a keyboard player, drummer, non-guitar-playing singer and guitar player.

Five or more: Endless possibilities, but the stage soon becomes crowded and transportation becomes a problem when you have this many people in the band.

Your band's lineup may change drastically anyway, as people come and go and decide they want to learn something new, so don't worry about it too much. The keyboard player might make some beautiful noises when he borrows the guitar player's Les Paul for a minute; if something like this happens, maybe they should switch instruments. Happens a lot.

Name Your Band. How many times have you been, like, reading a medical instruments catalog or the back of a can of corned beef hash and thought, *Whoa, that would be a great name for a band!* Somehow those names never quite suit your own band, and finding one that does may be a long and arduous process. Then, of course, you have to decide which wacky spelling to use. You might find and dismiss a thousand names before everyone agrees on the perfect one that symbolizes everything your band stands for and doesn't bring to mind any uncool musical things. Don't settle for a name you wouldn't wear on a T-shirt, but if you change your mind you can always change the name (and may have to if a band somewhere else already calls themselves Serving Suggestion).

Ally Yourselves. Next you need a posse. Every town in America with more than two local bands has a scene of some kind, a community of musicians and bands who hang out together. These little groups gossip and bitch like sororities or the Mafia, but they also share information and help one another. You must make these people your friends. They possess the knowledge you need to become a real working musician in your town.

Who you know is important, but not as important as who knows you. Favors will make a huge difference to your band's career—the photographer friend who'll take band pictures for free; the boss who'll be flexible with the work schedule. Without their good graces you're sunk. The whole music scene thrives on nepotism. Because so many bands of equal merit compete for the same slots, you have to give local decision-makers a reason to choose yours. Besides, a little niceness and intelligent conversation shows that you're not flaky like so many other musicians.

Now, with a band and a name and some support, you seem to be prepared, but before you proceed to higher levels of musical achievement, let's measure your attitude and tolerance of adversity.

Attitude Assessment Exam

The quiz below (I warned you!) will determine whether you are prepared to rock. Please circle True or False based on your feelings.

1. I want to be rich.   **T** F

2. I want to be famous.   **T** F

3. I want to receive free grilled cheese sandwiches at the local coffee shop and free beers when I go out.   T **F**

4. I want people to become nervous when they're near me.   T **F**

5. I want my name and "genius" in the same sentence.   T **F**

6. I want to complain about the fans and the journalists and the road.   T **F**

7. I have several years to waste working my ass off without seeing a dime.   T **F**

8. I am willing to be taken advantage of in every possible way (financially, sexually, etc.).   T **F**

9. I am prepared to alienate my friends and horrify my family.   T **F**

10. Sexually transmitted diseases don't frighten me.   T **F**

15

11. Sleep deprivation, malnutrition, and body odor cannot thwart me.   T / F

12. I have a few band names picked out already.   T / F

If you answered "False—no way!" for any of these questions, you failed the quiz, and you're not prepared to suffer enough for your art. (Oh, I'm just kidding!)

2

YARD SALE TODAY

(Instruments and Accessories)

NECESSARY MATERIALS: **None.**

ATTITUDE: **Eager and ready to learn OR wary and knowledgeable.**

FILTH FACTOR: **Pretty high, 6.**

DANGEROUSNESS: **Electricity and money are involved, so take the utmost care.**

OPPORTUNITIES FOR ROMANCE: **No more than on any other day.**

MUSICAL IMPORTANCE: **Significant. But expensive, delightful equipment is not necessary.**

PRICE: **How much do you have?**

TIME: **You can probably find something to play within a week, but instrument acquisition may become a lifetime hobby with some better, more beautiful item always just out of financial reach. Alas.**

POTENTIAL FOR HUMILIATION: **Pretty high.**

n this chapter we'll explore the wide world of wires, knobs, inputs, outlets, and technical details, but don't roll your eyes and start thumbing to funner chapters just yet. All the information has been abbreviated for your learning ease, with an overview of the accessories and toys that each little rocker in the band needs. And after it's all over, you'll be able to pace around after your show moodily whining about a failed cable or cracked tube, just like a real star.

Many musicians are really technicians who would rather discuss humbuckers than song structure; and guitar shops across the land staff themselves with such handy individuals. They love to share the wisdom as long as you listen in wide-eyed wonder. Keep them happy. You need to know the basic technical vocabulary because walking into a music store not knowing what you want is like walking into Piggly Wiggly and saying, "Excuse me, I'd like to buy some food." The commission-minded salesperson will immediately fill your cart with all kinds of junk you don't need. The non-commission salesperson won't even look up from his comic book.

Attitude Alert:

Opinionated Gearheads

You know that friend of yours who you never want to discuss music with because they take it very seriously, they know a lot, and they speak only in superlatives? ("It sucks!" "The most awesome..." "The absolute best...") Imagine he or she also possesses a mind-boggling amount of musical instrument trivia, and you've got a picture of the opinionated gearhead.

True life example: Some dude heard me talking about amps at a picnic. (Never saw the guy before in my life.) He jumped right in and said, "Of course, solid state amps are crap anyway, what you oughta do is get a tube amp, blah blah." He didn't know me, he didn't know what kind of music I liked, he didn't know what sound I wanted to achieve, he didn't know how much money I had or whether I was in a band, he didn't even ask what instrument we were talking about!

You will run into many of these people, because they own shops, produce records, and give lessons. They constantly foist opinions about gear on you, the easily confused beginner. They often add intimidation or embarrassment when you express ignorance about some simple thing. ("What *is* solid state? You seriously don't know what a solid state amp is? Oh, my God, really?!") And, of course, they are just dripping with attitude.

But, such people are not entirely evil. A real gearhead—as opposed to someone who is just full of shit—truly loves musical instruments and truly loves good sound.

Their intentions are pure and they often know a lot about the way things are made, how they work, where one can buy something, and what value a particular instrument has.

Don't let the attitude upset you and don't be embarrassed to form your own opinion based solely on aesthetics. When faced with an out-of-control gearhead getting all superior with the you-shoulds and you-ought-tos, call them out! Ask Mr. Head why he thinks solid state amps are so crappy if so many people use them—gosh, are those people crappy musicians? What's wrong with having a solid state amp and *liking* the way it sounds? A true gearhead will back up the opinion with fun facts about equipment and you might even learn something; whereas a mere bullshitter—well, you know what to expect from that person.

After reading this chapter, you will hold intelligent conversations with the technically advantaged and command respect at the music store with your mechanical wisdom. Additionally, you will earn the ardent love of your bandmates by familiarizing yourself with *their* equipment, too. So read the whole chapter.

Electric Guitar

WHAT IS IT?

A piece of wood (generally) with a long neck and strings stretched across it. Pickups make a guitar into an electric guitar.

HOW GUITARS AND BASSES WORK
(SEE FIGURE 2)

Noise starts with the string. Strike the guitar or bass string (1) and it vibrates (you can actually see it). Long strings vibrate at lower

20

FIG. 1. ELECTRIC GUITAR

Head Stock

Tuning Pegs (machine heads)

Nut

Inlays (sometimes of mother of pearl)

Strings (from left to right: E, A, D, G, B, E)

Frets and Fretboard

Body

Pick Guard

Pickup

Pickup

Tone & Volume Controls
(for the pickups)

Bridge

Input

Sunburst Finish (the paint job)

FIG. 2. MAKING NOISE

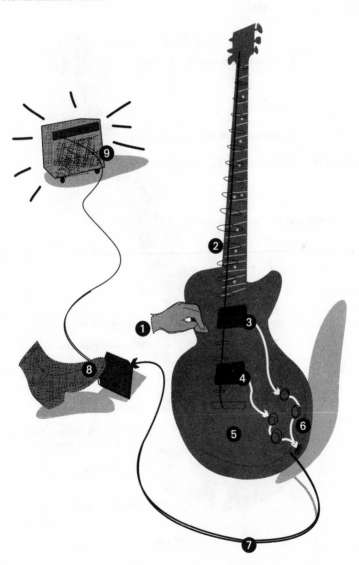

frequencies than short ones; when you press down on a fret you shorten the string and therefore make a higher note. Press at the 12th fret (the one with two dots) and you'll play the same note as the open string, one octave higher.

When you play the string, it vibrates most in the center (2), farthest from the bridge and nut, which hold it in place. The top pickup (3) will receive bassier frequencies and the one nearest the bridge (4) will receive treblier ones—same note, just different tones. The pickup translates those vibrations into electrical signals. Pickups are key! Good ones are very sensitive to the string's movement, but insensitive to outside noise; crappy ones will send all kinds of miscellaneous noise and buzzing and humming to the amp. Guitars and basses often have more than one pickup so that they produce a greater range of tones. The guitar's wiring (5) sends the signals out of the guitar. Tone knobs (6) allow you to vary the impulse as you play. Your cable (7) carries the signal to the amp. Effects pedals (8) alter the electrical impulses— and therefore alter the sound—before they reach the amp. The amp (9) changes the electricity back into mechanical energy—we call it noise.

Anyway, the main thing to know about pickups is whether they contain a single- or double-wrapped coil of wire. Double-wrapped are called humbuckers, and their extra coil of wire shields the pickup from outside noises and contains the frequencies that come from the vibrating string. Single-coil pickups are common in really old guitars.

Basic Model: Has six strings and two pickups. The guitar's sound comes from its strings, its pickups and then out of an amp, so the shape of the body—technically—is a little irrelevant. A heavy, solid body produces longer-sustaining notes and is generally agreed to be more rocking while the hollow body expresses more tone without the dramatic sustain and may feed back at very high volumes. Style and playing ease have really determined the shapes of solid-body electric guitars and basses more than anything else.

Variations: An acoustic guitar is the hollow kind with a hole: light-weight, friendly, and makes noise without an amp.

A twelve-string guitar has six pairs of strings positioned so that when you form chords, you actually press two strings with each finger instead of just one. Each pair of strings plays the same note as the single string on the regular guitar, but in some of the string pairs, one string is tuned an octave higher.

HOW DO YOU PLAY IT?

Watch a few videos, then use the fingers of one hand to hold down the strings while the other hand strums with a pick. Play chords by holding down and strumming more than one string at a time. Figure 9 (page 58) shows the exact fingerings for a few basic guitar chords.

Necessary Accessories: A strap, $15. A pick (unless your finger-nails are long and hardy); try thin or medium, or whichever color you like best, since they cost about a quarter each. A cable to connect your guitar to your amp, $15–$20. A set of extra strings, especially the smaller ones, which break often. A tuner; guitars and bass can share the same tuner, but someone in the band must have one, $60.

Unnecessary but Fun Accessories: Effects pedals alter the sound, causing it to echo or reverberate or whatever; and they have cool names like Death Metal, Classic Fuzz, and Big Muff. New ones cost like $60–$80.

Important Stereotype: *Guitar playing is sexy*. Admit it—in spite of the slouching posture, wrists bent at unnatural angles, and contorted faces, guitarists manage to attract people who wouldn't look twice if they saw them in the grocery store.

A Little Side Note for
the Overly Energetic

I know you probably look forward to engaging in all sorts of destructive rock behavior: swinging the microphone around by its cable (Rollinsing), kicking over the bass drum (Cobaining), punching holes in your Marshall stack with the head of your guitar (Townsending), then heaving your crazy self out into the crowd. Fun moments, to be sure, but not without a high price.

A brand new instrument from a reputable manufacturer will stand up to some lightweight abuse. Most won't. Guitars are so sensitive that a change in temperature can throw them out of tune; so imagine what happens when they bounce to the ground, headstock first. Yank the cables out of their inputs and you might loosen the wiring. Jostle your amp too hard and you could crack the tubes or (worse) break the transistors inside. Drop your cymbal bag and you could open it to find the ride chipped.

When you feel inclined to punkify your equipment, save your money and try some stupid stickers or a crappy paint job; and when the music moves you to leap into the crowd, *go for it*. Your body will heal.

Bass

WHAT IS IT?

Same as an electric guitar, really, but bigger.

FIG. 3. BASS GUITAR

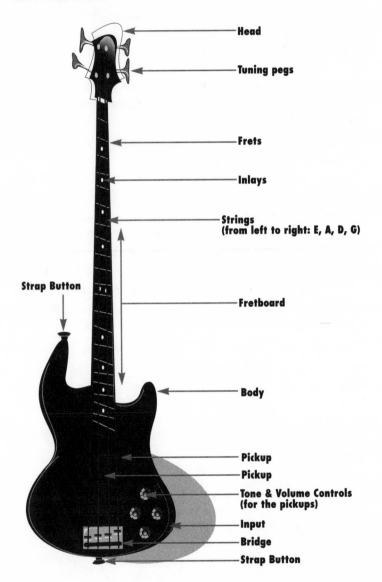

Head

Tuning pegs

Frets

Inlays

Strings
(from left to right: E, A, D, G)

Strap Button

Fretboard

Body

Pickup

Pickup

Tone & Volume Controls
(for the pickups)

Input

Bridge

Strap Button

Basic Model: Four chunky strings and a long neck. Bass strings are fatter than guitar strings and harder to press down. They rarely break, but every six months or so the threads fill up with finger grease and dirt. Then you replace them.

Variations: Five- (or even six-) string basses offer more notes to play, but the fretboard is wider and difficult to wrap your hand around, like the twelve-string guitar. The fifth string is usually a low B, but might be a high C on some older basses.

A short-scale bass features some guitar advantages: its shorter neck and closer-together frets allow you to easily reach trebley notes and play chords; and it weighs less than a full-scale bass. However, some short-scale basses lack the tonal depth because of their shorter strings and lighter-weight body.

Fretless basses resemble their stand-up cousins, but the fretboard has no marks, so remembering the notes is a bit more difficult. They have a different sort of sound, with more harmonics and more character.

HOW DO YOU PLAY IT?

*S*ame basic method as guitar playing, but the thick strings allow more ways to make the sound. Many bass players use a pick, but simply striking the strings will create noise, so fingers, thumb, and other parts of the hand can all be used. Go crazy.

Necessary Accessories: Like the guitarist, you need a strap and cable. Oh, and an amp.

Unnecessary but Fun Accessories: Effects pedals as with guitars. You can buy them especially for bass, or try guitar pedals.

Important Stereotypes: 1) *Bass players are tall, skinny, and funky*. The tall and skinny part has never been clinically proven. The funky concept may be left over from an era when band members wore

27

matching outfits on stage and choreographed their shows. Who knows? 2) *Bass players are short and stocky*. You can guess the shape of the person who told me this.

Bass players do serve a shifting function. As part of the rhythm section, they move the song along with the drummer; but as guitar players they contribute to the melody.

Brand-New Strings

If the bass or guitar you want to buy doesn't have strings on it, tell the person selling it to get their act together and string that thing up! (Unless you're at a yard sale, of course, then you're on your own.) You'll need help the first few times you string your guitar or bass, but if you want to fumble through it by yourself, here's how:

First, you gotta buy the right thing at the music store. Bass strings are different from guitar strings and acoustic guitar strings are different from electric guitar strings. (Fun fact: Electric guitar and bass strings are generally made of steel or nickel, while acoustic strings are made of copper or bronze.) Look on the envelope, it will tell you. Strings come in different weights, too: Super Light to Super Heavy, based upon their diameter. (Another fun fact: Thin strings have a higher pitch than thicker ones.) Lighter strings are easier to play, and that's good for you. Ask your friendly expert to recommend a brand, because you have many choices and in some cases, you may need an unusual style of string. Short-scale basses, for example, require special strings.

Do not begin by happily shearing the old strings off with wire cutters. You need them to show you how the last person did it (hopefully they knew what they were doing). Also, the tension of the strings holds the guitar in place in some ways, so the neck may bow or go wacky if it doesn't have that support. Oh, and don't open all the envelopes and scatter the new strings all over the floor because you won't be able to tell which one is which.

The guitar techs say you should do the middle two strings first and work your way out, but don't worry about that. Just choose one and either cut it with the wire cutters or unwind the peg until it falls out. Then pull it out from the bottom.

Feed the new strings up through the bottom whence the old one came so that its ball end anchors it. Then over the bridge, up the neck, and through the guides on the nut. Turn the tuning peg so that its slot or hole faces the bridge, and allows you to feed the string in without bending it. Leave enough slack to wind the string around the capstand two or three times. This is the tricky part. Expect to misestimate the amount of slack, since each string requires a slightly different amount. You may spend some time unwinding and rewinding the string a couple of times. Begin turning the peg to tighten the string, which should wind down from the hole or slot. Once the string has traveled around the peg twice, whip out that tuner and see what note comes out when you strike it. If the string plays something a little flat of the note you want to achieve, then you've done an exceptional job. (Seriously!) Tighten the string and make it perfect. If the note is nowhere in the neighborhood or if you've done a sloppy job, start over; don't be embarrassed to get professional help; and if you can, have someone check your work.

Fresh guitar strings relax quite a bit and go out of tune immediately, so you need to stretch them with a little massage. Firmly grab the string near the bridge, pull it away from the fretboard about a half inch or so, and slowly drag your hand down to the nut with a gentle, jerking motion so that you put pressure on the string's entire length and work the tension out of the whole thing. Tune the string, stretch it again, and retune. Then do the others.

FIG. 4. EFFECTS PEDAL

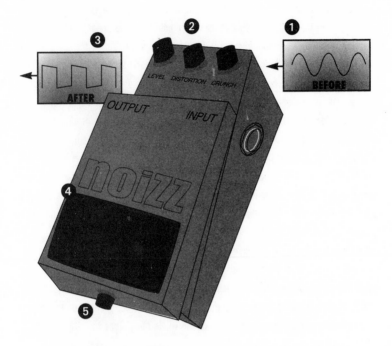

ACCESSORIZE WITH EFFECTS!

Simply, pedals alter sound waves by various forms of electrical magic. (Want more info than that? Ask your engineer or the geek you met earlier in the music store.) Use one on any instrument whose sound comes out of an amp, or use it with the microphone and PA to wackify vocals or miked instruments. You'll need an extra cable for each pedal that you use.

1) A cable brings the pure, curvy sine wave from your instrument to the pedal. 2) Effects pedals usually have a few controls: a volume knob determines loudness once the pedal's turned on, an application knob sets the amount of effect, and (sometimes) a tone control further hones the sound. 3) A second cable carries the altered signal to the amp, or to another effects pedal, a direct box, whatever. 4) Apply the effect by stomping here. 5) Unscrew this part to replace the 9-volt battery. The pedal depletes its battery any time the cable occupies the input jack, not only when you activate it, so don't leave your pedals lying around all set up.

Amplifiers—or ''Amps,''
As Those-in-the-Know Say

WHAT IS IT?

A wooden box with a speaker or a couple of speakers in it. Plug your guitar into the amp and sound comes out. Without one you are silent in a rock band.

Basic Model: Every amp has four sort of departments: *preamp, power amp, power supply,* and the *speaker* (technically, the amplifier and the speakers are two distinct entities, but never mind that). The *preamp* section receives the weak little voltage signal from the guitar and shapes it in a way unique to that amp. Tone knobs on the outside of the amp, such as *bass, treble*, and *presence*, control some of the preamp activity, and a *gain* or *volume* knob increases the signal. Turn the gain way up and the *master volume* down to hear the amp's natural distortion. The *power supply* brings the electricity in and transforms it to meet the amp's voltage needs. Then the *power amp* uses the electricity to boost the signals coming from the preamp, and sends them to the *speaker*.

Just as in the women's bathing suit department, there are two basic configurations. A *combo* (the one-piece) has everything in a single unit; and the two-piece consists of a *head and a cabinet*. The head is a little box that houses the preamp, power amp, and power supply. The cabinet contains the speaker. One type is no better than the other, except that amps are really heavy—get casters for the bottom or expect a hernia—and with a head, you can simply bring it to the show and use it with whatever cabinet you find there.

31

FIG. 5. HOW AN AMP WORKS

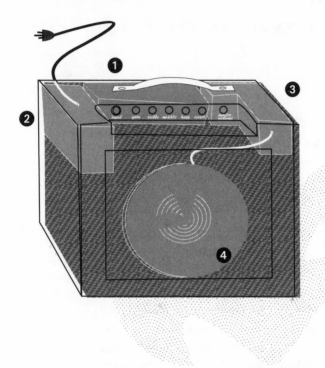

input   gain   treble   middle   bass   reverb   master volume

Plug your cable into the input, which brings the instrument's signal to the Preamp section (1). Use the Gain knob to turn that
signal way up and use the amp's distortion; use the other tone
knobs to shape the sound to suit you. The Power Supply (2) takes
electricity from the wall in your garage and changes it into the
voltage necessary to send the noise out big. The Power Amp (3)
boosts the signal created by the Preamp to the enormous levels
you deserve and sends it out to the Speaker or speakers (4).

Variations: Within the amp, electrical transfer happens one of two ways: with vacuum tubes or by transistor (also called solid state technology). Although I just can't bring myself to explain all the physics and chemistry that goes on inside there, you may encounter a lot of attitude about this technical difference. See, tubes are the old-fashioned way to make sound. Back in the day (like, before World War II), all radios, TVs, record players, PA systems, and amps used tubes, which would overheat during use and had to be replaced, just like light bulbs. What's worse, they often failed at really loud volumes. Solid state technology solved all three of those problems, plus it was cheaper, more reliable and not as heavy. In the early 1960s, transistors became the choice of amp manufacturers, but many musicians still preferred the sound of tube amps.

By now, solid state technology has replaced tubes everywhere except in some amps. You can find both solid state and tube amps, new and used, in addition to amps that combine both technologies. Bass amps almost always use solid state technology, but a lot of guitarists still prefer the tube sound; it's warmer, creates more depth, and the unpredictability creates more interesting feedback.

The construction of the speaker cabinet also affects the sound. An open-backed speaker cabinet (turn the amp around; can you see its insides?) allows the sound to come from the back of the amp as well as the front, like a lawn sprinkler; while an enclosed speaker gives more of a squirtgun effect, directional and more forceful.

HOW DO YOU WORK IT?

A cable carries the sound from the guitar or bass to the amp. Plug one end into your instrument and the other into the "input" on your amp, and turn it on to make noise. Use another cable to connect the head to the cabinet if your amp is in two pieces. Some amps may have two inputs or other places to plug into, like if two people want to play at the same time. This is good if you're in someone's living room or garage, working things out.

Because it's highly unlikely that you'll acquire a brand new amp, you'll have to rely on the amp's previous owner and your own experimentation to figure out which sounds you like best with your instrument. To introduce yourself to the amp, turn all the tone controls to the middle and see what happens to the sound when you adjust them one at a time. Many amps use different names for the same tone controls. The preamp may also be called *gain* or *input volume.*

Necessary Accessories: Cables.

Unnecessary but Fun Accessories: More amps, more wattage.

Important Stereotypes: 1) *Big amps = more noise, and noise is good.* Just as with football players, daintiness is not appreciated. However, many small amps produce big, beautiful sounds, and any amp can be miked to boost it to earsplitting levels. Like they say, "It's not the size of the ship..."

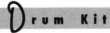

Drum Kit

WHAT IS IT?

It is not a box of drum pieces and a bottle of glue that you buy at Craft World.

Basic Model: The kit consists basically of drums and cymbals, and drummers can mix and match in any configuration to suit their taste. Bigger drums make lower-pitched booms than smaller ones, which go "bap" or "bhank." With cymbals, the mass affects the sound, so bigness, thickness, heaviness all make a difference. The cymbal's weight and size determine its sound.

FIG. 6. DRUM KIT

1. Ride cymbal.
2. Cymbal stand. (All of the stands, cymbals, legs, and other chrome parts are called hardware—put them into a bag and try to lift it, and you'll understand the name.)
3. Floor tom. (The drum's head—batter—is on top, that's the part you hit. Underneath, on the bottom, a resonator.)
4. Floor tom legs.
5. Rack toms.
6. Double tom holder.
7. Crash cymbal.
8. Hi-hat cymbals. A little piece called a clutch holds the top cymbal.
9. Hi-hat.
10. Bass (kick) drum.
11. Damper—in this case, an old pillow—to muffle the sound.
12. Bass drum pedal.
13. Snare drum and stand. See the snares across the bottom.
14. Rug scrap keeps everything from sliding around.

The bass drum is the big one, and you play it by stomping on a foot pedal that operates a mallet (use the sticks for all the other pieces). Little spurs on the sides keep it from rolling away. You have to dampen the bass drum's sound to keep it from making this enormous, out-of-control "boo-hoom." That's why you always see strange-looking things inside of the bass drum on stage. Any large, lightweight thing that'll absorb some of the sound: a winter coat, an old band uniform, a sofa cushion, a sleeping bag, a filthy pillow, a piece of car upholstery, some foam chunks, half a beanbag chair, a stained bedspread, etc.

The kit may have two types of tom-toms, rack toms and floor toms. A tom holder sticking out of the bass drum holds one or two rack toms. Rack toms look similar but one is actually smaller and has a higher sound than the other. The bigger floor tom, supported by its legs, has a deeper sound than the rack toms.

The snare drum resembles the one from marching band, with a row of coiled wires (called snares) across the bottom to create that splattering sound. It sits on a tripod stand that tilts it toward the drummer. The wires are very sensitive to vibrations, and guitar noise often rattles them even if the drummer is not playing—get used to that. (Fun fact: The snare drum is the only one that you'll find made out of metal. Not all snare drums are metal, but if you see a metal drum in the kit, it's either a snare or an oil can from the Caribbean.)

Ride and crash cymbals hang from individual stands so that they can move and vibrate. Both are available in different sizes, but generally the ride maintains rhythm and the crash creates the drama in the song. The hi-hat is a pair of cymbals mounted on a stand. Clap them closed with their foot pedal after striking to make a sssss-T noise.

Variations: Add or subtract these elements according to your finances or musical directives. The minimalist or rockabilly enthusiast may like to play just a bass, snare, and hi-hat, while the Lars Ulrich aspirant wants a second bass drum and floor tom and as many cymbals as she has room for.

HOW DO YOU WORK THESE THINGS?

Sit on the seat, hold the sticks in your hands, and let the magic begin. All of the pieces adjust to fit your size, including the seat. When you can comfortably reach everything, you're ready to play.

Unfortunately, your drums may not be ready for you to play them. Dented, broken, or just-not-there drum heads must be replaced. Your retailer should provide you with usable drum heads and put them on the drums. If you found your kit lying headless by the side of the road, take it to a music shop or have an experienced drummer help you put new heads on.

Then, just like a stringed instrument, the drums need to be tuned so that they emit nice sounds. Even though the drum head vibrates like a string does, it creates a variety of notes, so tuning it is a more subjective and difficult process than tuning a guitar. The drums don't achieve precise musical notes, so there's no mechanical system to help you tune them. Instead, you judge for yourself about the quality of the sound, and try to get a variety of pitch from the different drums (you don't tune the cymbals) in your kit.

Alter the tautness of the head by adjusting the tension rod with a drum key. First, make a series of light taps with the stick around the perimeter of the head so you will hear discrepancies in its tautness. Fix these with small turns of the key where you find them so that you get the same noise from the drum no matter where you hit it. Then listen to the drums in comparison to one another. If your two rack toms sound alike, you may want to tighten one and raise its pitch a bit so that you get a greater variety of sounds from the kit. Anyway, tuning the drums is tough, so if you can find someone to help you do it every once in a while, take advantage of their skills; or have your friendly retailer tune them and show you how to do it.

Necessary Accessories: Sticks, about $6 per set, and a piece of carpeting to put under the set, which prevents the pieces from moving out of reach as you beat on them.

Unnecessary but Fun Accessories: Sizzles are these things that go on the cymbals to give them a ringing sound; different types of sticks also give the sound different qualities; and of course accessories like a cowbell or tambourine add something special.

Important Stereotypes: 1) *Drummers are easily replaced.* Drummers do not receive the esteem they deserve. They are not usually considered to be part of the songwriting process, yet the band totally depends upon their perfection. A sloppy guitarist can get away with "eccentric," but a sloppy drummer just sucks. Their equipment is heavy and there's tons of it. They sit at the back of the stage and sweat buckets in the dark and no one wants to kiss them after the show. They're still packing up while dewy-faced guitarists and singers collect adulations and free drinks. 2) *Drummers possess a wild side—an animal magnetism—that other musicians lack.* Yeah, well you have only to watch a drummer's face during his/her set to see that this is true. One can't help but wonder, "What would happen if I asked this passionate, physically adept, sweating object-of-desire back to my place for a shower?" Someone must do some research on the topic.

Microphone and PA

WHAT ARE THEY?

Like an amp for the vocals, the PA (which stands for public address system) is actually several pieces of equipment: a *mixer*, an *ampli-*

FIG. 7. MICROPHONE AND PA

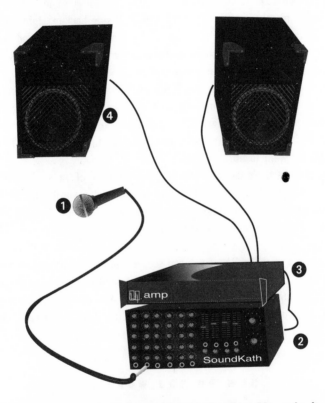

A microphone (1) picks up the signal and a cable carries it to the mixer. The mixer (2) provides volume and tone controls for each of the inputs; you can create a balance between band members who sing at different levels, and you can add effects where you want them. The amplifier (3) adds power to the signal and sends it to the speakers (4) so you can hear your awesome singing. P.A. stands for public address system, a totally generic term that could mean the system that the Principal uses to announce whose busses are going to be late. For us, it means the system that amplifies the vocals.

fier, and *speakers*. Plug the microphones into the mixer and they send the sound to a set of speakers.

Basic Model: Has at least four inputs—one for you and a few more for other members of the band. (You will all sing backup, right?) Each input has a set of knobs to control its individual sound, and some controls for the overall volume and sound quality. At any club or by-the-hour rehearsal space, your vocals will go through a PA.

With or without a PA, you'll need a microphone. Your *own* microphone. Otherwise, imagine climbing onstage after six other lovelies who've been spitting angry lyrics into the mike all night, smearing it with lipstick and clutching it in sweaty palms. Just the smell of it will make you want to hurl.

Most of the mikes you will encounter outside of the studio will be basic, do-everything mikes. If you're buying, get a vocal mike (made specifically for human singing) as opposed to a mike for the bass drum or a music video prop or something.

Variations: The PA, as you can see, is a big deal. It's expensive and technical. Until you have the cash and the total dedication to your band, you can plug your mike directly into an amp. You won't sound so great, and your amp might not appreciate it, but do it until you can afford something designed for vocals.

HOW DO YOU WORK IT?

Since the PA is actually a system of different pieces of equipment, someone should help you learn the basics of its operation. The system works on the same basic principles as an amp and guitar, however.

Necessary Accessories: When you do get a PA, you'll need some kind of rack to shelve its components that allows you to plug things into the back and front. The speakers work best when hanging from the ceiling, so that their sounds hit your head. A microphone needs a cable to send its signal to the mixer or to the amp. XLR is the name of the cable's prong connection that fits into the mic, and at the other end is another XLR for the PA, or a ¼-inch plug for an amp.

Unnecessary but Fun Accessories: You need a microphone stand if you plan to sing and play simultaneously, otherwise hold it the whole time, like Tom Jones, or tape it to your face.

Keyboard

WHAT IS IT?

Well, an *electric piano* has hammers inside like its unplugged parent, but it also has the technology to amplify the sound when it's plugged into an amp. Each key has a little pickup inside to change the noise into an electric signal. An *electronic piano* reproduces piano sounds and amplifies them. A *digital piano* or *digital keyboard* does the same, just with digital technology and often using internal samples. An *organ* is not a stringed instrument or a reproduction of one. Organs have stops that you turn on or off to create tones. Use more stops to thicken the sound. A *Hammond-style organ* sends air from the speakers through spinning pipes. It weighs a ton and you probably won't find such a thing useful for playing out. An *electronic organ* reproduces the original organ sounds, but because its stops are electronic, like effects pedals on a guitar, the organ makes many wack noises and distorts in a very cool way.

Synthesizers allow you to create sounds, and the keys give you control over playing them back. Newer models use digital technology, and the little ones that you'll likely encounter at yard sales don't allow you to decide what to synthesize, but instead have a bunch of preset noises. Whatever kind of keyboard you find, if you can lift it by yourself,

FIG. 8. KEYBOARD (TOP)

Rhythm Selections

Recording/Memory Functions

Tone Selections

Speakers

Master Volume

Speakers

Keys

Stand

(BACK)

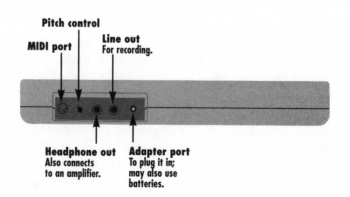

Pitch control

MIDI port

Line out
For recording.

Headphone out
Also connects
to an amplifier.

Adapter port
To plug it in;
may also use
batteries.

it's probably one of those—no strings, no ivory, no pipes. It can make many different noises, keep time, and remember what you've played. Even the most rudimentary of these little keyboard synthesizers comes in handy as a songwriting tool.

Basic Model: Has a range of tones, or instrument sounds, to choose from (often very strange in the older models); a selection of rhythms; and a memory function that will help you compose songs.

Variations: Keyboard manufacturers constantly reinvent their instrument as new technology develops, so variations abound. Older keyboards have fewer functions, and their limited capacity gives them a unique sound. Some of their sounds are so distinct that you can name the old records that feature a particular kind of keyboard just by hearing it. Bands with amplified keyboards didn't really happen until like, the sixties, and back then the high-tech keyboards were voltage-controlled. They created sound by generating an electrical current using oscillators and then shaping it by filtering out certain frequencies (like the tone knobs or effects on a guitar). The keyboard player couldn't program them and they didn't always stay in tune.

By the mid-eighties, digital synthesizers came along: cheap, lightweight, and basically infallible because their computer technology creates sound by imitating the wave forms of other instruments. Synthesizers offered so many sound options and were so easy to use that they immediately influenced the music of the time. Soon MIDI (musical instrument digital interface) was developed to allow musicians to control other instruments, including keyboards or drum machines (the subject of many other books).

The more money you spend, the more a keyboard will do: produce a four-track recording, sample other sounds, help you practice with its preprogrammed tunes, and keep your lovely compositions in its memory.

HOW DO YOU WORK IT?

Took ballet instead of piano? Don't worry, a keyboard doesn't have as many keys (sometimes as few as 45), and you can program it to do a lot of the work for you. The little at-home keyboards usually have a speaker built in, so you don't need an amp to practice, but the speaker's not loud enough for playing live; plug it into an amp for live shows. Write to the manufacturer if you need more information about the old garage-sale model you bought. They often have copies of the original instruction manuals that they can send to you.

Necessary Accessories: You may need an AC adapter to power the keyboard, and the usual cables if you want to hear the sound through an amplifier.

Unnecessary but Fun Accessories: A sequencer will help you to actually compose songs with the keyboard, or you can buy software to use with your personal computer so that it will remember a complicated series of notes, volume changes, effects, and the rest. So much stuff is available for keyboards—drum machines, guitar synthesizers, piano synthesizers, samplers, sound boxes—that I won't even bother to list them all. You can, however, use the keyboard with your guitar pedals to get some really wack noises.

Other Instruments

LIKE WHAT?

Accordion, flute, saxophone, banjo, violin, harmonica, cello, bagpipes, you name it.

44

HOW DO YOU WORK IT?

Anything that makes noise can make an important creative contribution and can be adapted to playing live. Hollow instruments, like a violin or acoustic guitar, can be outfitted with an output jack so their sound goes directly to the amp, like with an electric guitar or bass.

Use a microphone and amp to boost the sound of everything else. Mikes sit on their stands for horn players, who just blow right into them like a vocalist would. Accordions and bagpipes, since they move when you play them, may require a customized microphone attachment.

Enough equipment! As you become familiar with your instrument of choice, you'll make your own much longer list of "necessary accessories." You will also learn about equipment by watching other musicians play at shows, by asking questions and by flipping through catalogs and magazines. When you go to see a band, sidle up to the stage and check out the setup. After the show, don't be shy. Ask the wise band member about pedals or cymbals or anything. Maybe he or she will give an impromptu lesson or let you borrow that special item.

Before you rush out to Hey Dude Music Shoppe with all your new knowledge and Mom's credit card, get ahold of as much gear as possible the old-fashioned way—borrow it. Ask around to see who has old equipment, and you'll be surprised at the unlikely characters who drag guitars from their closet or a drum kit from the basement. Your local rock connoisseur/guitar collector might have something to lend, as might any stable, older folks who may have gone through a "rebellious" phase, like your nerdy, marketing analyst cousin. Definitely hit friends of Mom or Grandma up for stuff. Older folks whose kids have moved out will love it if you take rock 'n' roll equipment off their hands: "Oh, the racket that Tube Screamer made. I know he hasn't played it since he got married. You sure can have it, sweetie, just as long as your mother says it's OK."

If the generous older ladies have already been tapped dry, borrow stuff from your peers. Actually, borrowing is a good idea even if you already have an instrument to play. The more equipment you handle, the more you'll know about what you'd like to eventually play. By borrowing, you can experiment with different sounds and get the real pros and cons about the instrument from its owner.

When it comes time to really spend the bucks, a used instrument will usually serve your early rocker purposes better than some brand new thing. A good guitar or amp will play just as well twenty years after its manufacture. Consider the number of Bruce Springsteen and Black Sabbath wannabes over the decades who've needed some quick cash, and you've got used music stores and pawnshops across the country stocked with cheap, playable instruments.

Shopping for musical instruments can be pretty intimidating, though. Even the most experienced, rockin' musicians I spoke to agreed that salespeople often lack a certain, shall we say, open-mindedness. The dude with the really tight black jeans might not be too psyched when you interrupt his conversation with the Danzig lookalike to ask a simple question. Be patient, have some sense of humor, and *don't let them overlook you*. Once you've located the helpful, knowledgeable salesperson, confess: "I'm looking for a new guitar and maybe an amp, I'm a beginner and I like the sound of my friend's Stratocaster (or whatever); can I try some things?" Never, ever buy anything until you've played it yourself a couple of times. It helps a lot to bring someone with you who knows about instruments and who can, like, nudge you and whisper in your ear, "Ask if you can play it" or "Ask whether it's ever been repaired." Prices for used equipment are often negotiable, so boldly suggest a deal.

Don't feel like you must buy an instrument immediately. If you've borrowed and begged enough gear to get started, don't worry if the setup is not exactly what you want. Start making music, that's more important. Two acoustic guitars and a snare drum is better than nothing, and it's enough equipment to write a song. Instruments will find their way into your hands just like cats find their way to the crazy lady's house.

Chris Cush sells guitars and amps and basses and strings and a few other things—mostly used—out of Mojo, his New York City shop that's like half the size of a suburban mud room. He knows a lot and he helped me compile these.

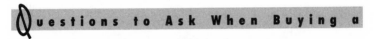

Questions to Ask When Buying a Used Guitar

How much can I spend? If you only have $75 in the piggy bank, guitar shopping might be difficult, but don't let that stop you. A lot of instruments out there are only *worth* $75. Whatever number you come up with, stick to your budget, because you can always spend more money later. For you credit card holders—well, you know your weaknesses—a budget is still a good idea.

Will you be my date? Recruit a guitar geek or bring your teacher to help you with the vocabulary, ask questions, and look at things.

Is that a guitar or a bass? Hook up with the friendly salesperson. Explain your budget and ask to try some things. Check out the items in your price range, especially those with familiar name brands. Ask any question that comes to mind. A good shop, Chris says, won't give you any attitude for asking dumb questions and will patiently explain stuff to you. Don't be embarrassed.

Why is there this big hole in it? Check for things that don't line up properly, bad workmanship, big cracks or excessive wear. Peek inside each of the drums. If any part of the instrument strikes you as unusual or crappy-looking, ask about it. You might notice marks made by a part that's no longer there; but the new part might be much better—get the story from the salesperson.

47

Can you take it down for me? It might seem like kicking the tires of a used car, but Chris recommends that you give the thing a good shake. Loose and rattling parts are a bad sign. "Hey," Chris points out, "the pickup might fall out or something. If it doesn't withstand a good shaking, what'll happen when you jump up and down with it on stage?"

Why is it making that weird noise? Does it feel good when you play it? Can your fingers press down the strings easily? Does each note sound OK? Your tag-along expert should also play it. Listen for buzzing noises when you play certain notes, when you tap the top of the instrument with your finger, or any other kind. Buzzing is bad.

Hey, can you throw in a hard case? If you like the sound and the price is right, whip out that wallet and take it home today. Be nervy. Ask the salesperson to throw in a case and a strap and a couple of picks. Oh, and lunch! Get lunch too.

General Warnings: *Great deals can be had when you buy from someone who wants to unload their equipment, and most musicians get their first instruments from other musicians. Unfortunately, they could rip you off much easier than any retailer could. See if your local store has something similar to what the unloader is offering. "People often have strange ideas about quality and originality," Chris warns cryptically.*

3

Y E OLDE BASEMENT

(Principles and Practice)

NECESSARY MATERIALS: A band and instruments.

ATTITUDE: Hard work and harmony.

FILTH FACTOR: Garages and basements are grubby.

DANGEROUSNESS: You risk falling in love with your music, neglecting your studies, destroying your chances for a "real" career, and spending the most important years of your life sleeping until noon. That's all.

OPPORTUNITIES FOR ROMANCE : Sorry.

MUSICAL IMPORTANCE: Very great.

PRICE: Free, for most of you.

TIME: As long as you want.

POTENTIAL FOR HUMILIATION: Pretty low, for once.

guess that a plan for rock success would include some kind of guide to technical proficiency—directions for operating your chosen rock instrument and a bunch of exercises and lessons. Whether you use your voice or clank a cowbell, someone somewhere has very serious ideas about how to do it correctly. Chapter 3 here would be the guidelines and rules chapter, with lots of diagrams showing where to place your fingers, directions for proper breathing, a long section on reading music, and maybe a few worksheets and shit.

Uh, yeah. While somebody somewhere might feel strongly about how you should clank the cowbell, I don't; and I don't care about reading music either. The only people I know who read music are the ones who always get summoned to the piano at Christmastime. To construct a lesson plan would spoil that do-it-yourself energy that's driving the whole of you to play music, and would just bore everyone involved. But alas, you must learn or *you will forever suck;* so try the painless, back-door route described here for learning to play and rehearse.

TEACH YOURSELF

*E*arn your musical status in the comfort of your own home. First, acquire an instrument to call your own (singers already have one). Fall madly in love with the thing, become obsessed with your new potential for making music, and play constantly. You will learn the most by just spending hours with your hands on the prized item, experimenting to make various sounds come out of it. Work alone or with the band.

LEARN WITH A TEACHER

*O*K, I'll confess a little fear that I have. When you sit before an instrument that you know nothing about, you will learn to play in a style that is uniquely yours. Physical limitations *(ouch, can't reach it—I'll hit this one)* and personal taste *(sounds cool!)* will guide your playing and writing. But when you encounter an instrument with a bunch of ideas about how music *should* sound *(OK, songs have an introduction, then a verse and a chorus),* or what patterns of noises you should be making, your mind automatically goes there and you stunt your creativity.

Teachers focus your attention on what they believe is the right way to make music; that's what teaching is all about. Unfortunately, in that process they sometimes close their minds—and yours—to other ideas. (Not only do teachers often adhere to a definitive right and wrong, but many musicians do, too.) What if your teacher prevents you from doing something cool? I know a guitar player, for example, whose guitar is actually a bass. He puts lighter gauge strings on it and plays through a trebley amp to achieve a very fat guitar sound. It's cool, but a teacher would freak if you showed up for a lesson with a four-stringed guitar. I also know a great bass player who produces some really sick sounds by dragging a big saw across her bass. Imagine if she had shown up at the music school with a toolbox? Lefty Jimi Hendrix played his guitar upside down, for crying in the sink!

Although it may annoy your sense of artistry to be taught how to *play*, it benefits you to get as much operating instruction for your instrument as possible. Once you become familiar with all of its components and experience the range of noises it can make, you will have more fun playing. A good teacher can quickly impart lots of this type of basic technical information; show you five-minute shortcuts or tricks that would take you years to figure out on your own; and make your playing or singing more efficient. A great teacher knows a ton of information about your instrument, plays really well, wants to listen to music with you, and will show you how to achieve certain sounds. She also understands that the whole process is about creativity and fun, not about adhering to some laws.

Go to your little lessons; if the wise old owl with the Grace Slick hair bores you or force-feeds you too many Beatles songs, either hang on for the good parts—you can learn something from anyone—or find a cooler Miss Crabtree.

BOOKS

Many very nice books have been published that go into detail about rock technique; and I insist that you trot down to your library and look at the ones they have there. Not only might these books contain some informative text, but often they also contain particularly amusing photos of, like, rock greats from the sixties wearing high-heeled fur boots, and a novice like yourself can learn some important fashion and posing techniques.

For references that don't predate your birth, the bookstore and music store also have lots of books that can help you learn specific techniques. Take a look at all of these books, even if you don't like the tacky picture on the front cover.

GEARHEAD MAGAZINES

The magazines are far more embarrassing than the books, because they feature all the same rock greats of the sixties, sporting acid-wash jean vests and long, grayish, frizzy hairdos. These magazines usually take a typical, macho rock outlook, but they enlighten with lots of pictures, reviews of new equipment, and interviews with artists about what they play.

VIDEOS

More amusing than the books—hilarious, even; don't shun the instructional videos just because of their cheesy cover photos or silly titles. In a video, unlike a book, you'll see where the hands go and hear the result. You could learn something from Billy Sheehan! Singers *may* find instructional videos or cassettes at the library, but the rest of you have to shell out; and I have to honestly admit that I've never seen one of these videos because they cost anywhere from $40 to $100.

CATALOGS

Lots of companies sell gear by mail. Hook yourself up with their catalogs and you'll have a reference that gives you a picture, a description, and a price—good for comparisons when you shop, or just to help learn to identify different pieces of equipment.

WHY STOP THERE?

A person who calls herself an instructor ain't the only person to learn things from. Watch other people play. Stand right up front at the show and watch the arms and legs and mouth and fingers. See something strange? Ask the musician what they did.

Put on your CDs and listen to how other people play rhythm, put notes together, and structure their songs. Think about re-creating bits and pieces from songs that you like, to exercise your fingers, or to consider different ways of strumming, drumming, vocalizing, whatever.

Time for Some Science

Notes and scales? Who cares?; but Hertz and kiloHertz, now there's some fascinating stuff. Vibration is sound; place your hand over your throat or on the stereo's speaker cone to feel the wobbling and throbbing producing the sound wave that has already reached your ears (traveling at a rate of about 5 seconds per mile). The rate of vibration determines the pitch you hear—faster makes a higher pitch, slower makes lower pitch. Mr. Heinrich Hertz devised a system to measure the rate of vibrations, and of course, he named his units Hertz—Hz for short. The greater the frequency of vibrations, the higher the Hz of the tone you hear and the higher the pitch of that particular sound.

Things that make noise, including musical instruments, emit a variety of Hz levels, or tones. Hit a wineglass with a spoon or touch a piano string, for example, and you hear a single musical note out of both of them—D, let's say. But a wineglass doesn't sound like a piano, even if they produce the same musical note; because both of these instruments actually creates a whole bunch of different overtones which harmonize to give the sound you hear its distinctive character. In these two cases, the cumulative sound happens to fall conveniently within our familiar musical scale. Each note on that scale has a specific Hz: the A above middle C produces 440 Hz, and the next A, one octave higher, produces 880 Hz, while the lower A produces 220 Hz, etc.

The presence of overtones explains why you may hear different notes when you play two pure tones at once. Play an E (333 Hz) and a C (528 Hz) at the same time and many people will also hear a third note, the G (528 − 333 = 195 Hz).

Most sounds we hear have no relationship at all to that scale. When you tear a sheet of paper in half or hit a snare drum, your instrument still produces a wide range of tones and overtones that characterize the sound, but these sounds don't harmonize in a nice and neat way to produce a single musical note.

Our fallible human ears can only hear a fraction of the possible frequencies—those that fall between about 16 Hz and 20 kHz (20,000 Hz)—and most music uses an even more limited range of frequencies: 27 Hz to about 15 kHz.

Why do I bore you so? This sort of nerdily numerical information helps when you buy speakers, think about earplugs, and use any kind of equalizer. It'll come in handy, I promise.

*R*ehearsal

Before you go any further, you gotta find someplace to leave all your junk where it will be safe and you can be loud. Your parents or room-mates probably hate your noisy ass already, but if you can't afford to move to private quarters, a little soundproofing may restore their love.

Most of you are surrounded by real estate that allows for dirt-cheap or free rehearsal space: garages, basements, or backyard barns. City dwellers don't have it so easy. Some cities have a few places where you can rent space by the hour, or actually sign a lease and rent the place like an apartment. Find out how all the other bands you know do it and keep your ears open for a good sharing situation. When a band breaks up or goes on tour, rehearsal space becomes available. Act fast.

Extra layers of anything thwart the decibels, but old carpet scraps or big slabs of acoustic foam (if the budget allows) thwart best and hang easiest. Of course, you need a good rumpus-room, clubhouse kind of vibe in your rehearsal space—a few naughty pictures on the wall, inspirational bric-a-brac like a neon beer sign, garbage in the corners, and a beanbag chair complete the look. Send Martha Stewart a photo so she can feature the place in an upcoming issue of her magazine. When you finish decorating you may want to work on some music.

Remember: *Practice* is not rehearsal. Practice happens at home, when you are teaching your fingers or throat some new trick and need to just do it over and over again. The band won't appreciate you making them wait while you stand there going over your new part forty-five times because you haven't learned it yet. Work that shit out at home or just show up a little early for rehearsal and do it then. Rehearsal happens when you go over your songs or just play them together, talk about the snags, and work things out as a group. Although you usually have fun writing new songs, jamming, and making noise, rehearsal is work.

Often a lot of musically not-so-productive things happen. People bring their problems to the band and instead of writing music, you talk instead of playing. Well, so? If your band becomes the quilting bee of the neighborhood, and you write some music, play a few songs, and talk about why Ms. X would want to go out with Mr. Y when so many other worthy individuals exist, like serial killers and gas station attendants, who's to care? Just so long as everyone can deal with that pace. On the other hand, some rehearsals go like football practice, with hard work for hours and no rest. It doesn't matter how you like to do it. Obviously you accomplish more by playing constantly, but a relaxed rehearsal will more likely produce a cool new song, and develop a good habit of patiently working through things together. And there's nothing wrong with a just plain lazy atmosphere.

Try to keep unpleasant impulses under control. If you've had a particularly shitty day at the bagel counter and don't feel like standing around in a freezing-cold basement with your stupid band, just warn everyone when you arrive that Satan has invaded your body—and lay low.

*M*ethodology

1. SOME NICE CHORDS FOR GUITARISTS

Sure they're tricky, but learn just three of them and you've written a song; and besides, you can usually bang all of the strings when you play a chord. On the following page, I've diagrammed 22 common chords that you can use to make some noise and exercise your fingers. This is only the tip of the chord iceberg. There are thousands of chord possibilities, and always more than one way to make a certain sound; so you have a lot of room to experiment and create your own. Try putting your fingers different ways and make up your own configurations. They will probably sound cooler than my dorky collection of pickin' and grinnin' favorites anyway.

The horizontal lines on the diagrams represent frets, the numbers represent your fingers. Press the strings with the fingers and strum to hear the chord. Where a string is represented by a dotted line, don't play it. See, not hard at all.

I haven't included any barre chords because they're a bit tricky, but they create some really cool sounds. You form the barre chords by pressing down all the strings with one finger, and using others to form the chord; then, you move your whole hand as you strum to hit different chords. Have your guitar expert teach you a few when your fingers are ready.

2. SOME NICE CHORDS FOR BASS PLAYERS

Just so you don't feel left out here's a little chord lesson for bass players, too. They're a bit more challenging because the frets are further apart and the strings tougher to keep steady.

FIG. 9. CHORDS FOR GUITARISTS

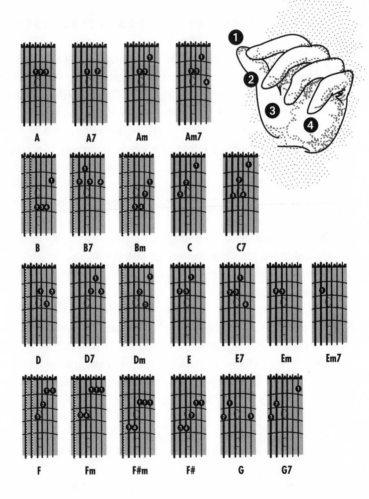

A   A7   Am   Am7

B   B7   Bm   C   C7

D   D7   Dm   E   E7   Em   Em7

F   Fm   F#m   F#   G   G7

Words from an Expert: *Plenty of bass players don't play chords because if not done tastefully it can make your music sound muddy. There are all kinds of complex chords on the bass, but here's a sure-fire method to form a chord. Finger a note, say an F, on the E-string with your index finger. Now go to the A-string and put your ring finger two frets up on the note C. This note is called the "fifth." Now go to the D-string and put your pinkie on the same fret your ring finger is on. This is also an F, but it is one octave above your low F. Now strum away on the three strings and you're playing a chord! And it works in any starting position on the neck.*

The picture shows the sure-fire method. Using the E, A, and D strings or the A, D, and G strings, you create chords in any position along the fretboard. Just as with guitar chords, the possibilities for interesting noise never end. Try your own variations.

FIG. 10. BASS CHORDS

4

IT GOES A LITTLE

SOMETHING LIKE THIS

(Writing Songs)

NECESSARY MATERIALS:

Instruments, if you have any.

Band members, if you want to play with them.

A tape recorder or notebook.

ATTITUDE: Relaxed and open-minded.

FILTH FACTOR: Minimal, 1 out of 10.

DANGEROUSNESS: Aside from potential bickering, none.

OPPORTUNITIES FOR ROMANCE: Don't get carried away, we're here to work.

MUSICAL IMPORTANCE: Paramount.

PRICE: No money should change hands.

60

TIME: A relative concept for this chapter.

POTENTIAL FOR HUMILIATION: Astronomical—you'll be revealing your deepest
feelings to the world, right?

Years from now, when you've reached paunchy middle age, when Alice in Chains and Metallica have achieved dinosaur status on oldies stations, your children will refuse to believe you were a rebellious little rocker. "No way," they'll argue in the cruel way that children have, "you're too into kung fu movies and golf to have ever been a cool person." The only thing that can save your reputation will be the songs you wrote and some hilarious photos. The photos will prove them right, but good songs will always fell the skeptic.

The other aspects of band life hardly suffer at all if you approach them lazily. Your image, for example: if you don't feel like changing clothes between your bakery job and your show, and get onstage wearing a stained apron and mismatched socks, only your mother will mind. And your promotional efforts don't always have to be perfect either; if you send out invitations with the wrong date because you couldn't be bothered to double check, people will get over it. But people won't get over lame tunes; they won't stay to hear them and may never come to another of your shows again if that's what the band plays.

The songs are the most important part of band life, they're the one way that you can impress a listener since you don't have the technical skill or the experience that other musicians may have. Creative songwriting is far more important than anything else the band does. The person who simply plays well but does not create is called a drummer or singer or whatever; but a person who writes is called an artist—and don't forget it, man! Besides, technical aptitude and experience will come with time. The songs you write will represent you better than any picture or logo or rumor. They prove that you were in the band, and they will last long after your hair grows back to its natural color.

So, even though your band's existence hinges on these songs, that's no reason to get all aggravated and start thinking seriously about the songwriting process. Thankfully, you will have more fun writing than doing most band stuff. A good, groovy feeling makes a huge difference between the fun and the chore. To get started and develop the right mindframe, choose a place to write that's comfortable, where everyone can relax with whatever food or beverage they prefer, and just hang out acting loud and ugly. Pretend that you have all the time in the world and no one wants to interrupt you for any reason. Oh, and bring an instrument if you have one.

All bands work differently when it comes to making masterpieces, but you will probably find that you create songs in two phases. The first phase involves playing: with creative juices flowing, you come up with bits and pieces of music and decide that you like them enough to make a song out of them. The second phase is about listening, and organizing the bits with the pieces so that the thing has a design and everyone knows what to play. You can write alone or with the rest of your band, whenever you feel inspired.

63

Phase 1

You could call it jamming, just making noise to see what happens. Like a stream of musical consciousness, you just play, see what happens, and come up with riffs and rhythms that will become the song. The key is to just mess around, keep an open mind, and be ready for the cool things that will happen by accident. Try anything that comes into your head, even things from other songs.

With others: With the rest of your band, songs happen organically, they just sort of grow like mold as you play together. One or two of you may start together, the others join, and after a while everyone starts to play something cool, then people get bored or experiment a little with a different beat or chord, and the whole thing changes again. Simply picking up your instrument with other musicians will inspire fabulous melodies, and songs will happen without much thought to how it's happening or whether it's the sound you want or who it sounds like. Just let the noise come out. Play any idea at all that you have, and definitely don't feel embarrassed. Even if you have a corny or otherwise uncool idea in your head, play it anyway. The really exciting thing about playing with other people is that they come up with totally different ideas, and your corny melody may be completely transformed by their interpretation and contribution.

Don't expect the genius songwriting sessions to flow freely, though. Sometimes you'll play for five minutes and come up with something everyone loves. Other times it just doesn't happen at all; if a bad vibe or bad mood has pervaded rehearsal, just let it pass.

Throughout this chapter, I've included professional-proven methods for writing songs. No rules, as usual, but try not to fight among yourselves or get too stressed out if things don't always work.

SPECIAL PROCESS FOR GUITARISTS I

1. First one to get their guitar out works some riff while the others smoke cigarettes (*your author doesn't recommend the smoking part*) and tune their guitars.

2. Drummer joins in.

3. After about 1½ minutes, the first guitarist is sick of these four notes but someone says, "That's cool, keep playing it."

4. The first guitarist, who now hates it, says, "I don't remember what I was playing, can we work on something else?"

   Steps 1–3 will happen many many times in your musical life, and provide satisfactory song parts for all.

SPECIAL PROCESS FOR GUITARISTS II

1. Guitar #1 sits in the corner playing her favorite Nirvana song.

2. Bass player, not recognizing it, begins a non-Novoselic bass line.

3. Drummer, singer, and guitar #2, assuming that this is a brand new song, invent new parts to accompany the other two.

4. Someone says, "That's great! We should open with it at our next show. What should we call it?"

5. Guitar #1 says, "It's called 'Heart Shaped Box,' you dorks!"

6. Guitar #2 says, " 'Heart Shaped Box' doesn't go like that, it goes like this" (strum strum).

7. The band has a fight about "Heart Shaped Box," then calls their new song "Box Shaped Heart."

(Actually, a lot of cool riffs may come from your lame, unskilled attempts to play someone else's music, because you might be playing it really slow or only playing part of what they play, or even have switched instruments without realizing.)

The inspired singer might choose a couple of important phrases to help her remember melody ideas or capture the overall feeling for the song. Usually these lyrics are sketchy and their writer will finish them after listening to the song a few more times. *Lalalas* and *Ohs* may be enough to help you remember what and where you wanted to sing.

As you write the song, you probably won't pay any more attention to the lyrics than you do to the instruments' parts. A few phrases or noises will come out during the Phase I jam; and as you put the song together in Phase II, you'll figure out which parts of the song should have singing and which parts will be instrumental.

People who hear your music relate more to the lyrics than, say, to the drum part, so your lyricist has to think about her contribution differently than any instrumental part. The drums can definitely evoke a mood or excite the song in a special way that the vocals can't, but no one will listen to the drummer and wonder which of her failed relationships has inspired her drum part—the singer has to deal with that kind of scrutiny.

Good lyrics come from truly personal feelings; they come directly from your emotion-filled brain and don't mimic anyone else's wording or style. They don't necessarily have to reflect misery, loss, and melodrama, but they have to reflect you. Whether the words make you sad, make you laugh, exact homicidal revenge, or tell a story, every line should relate personally to you.

You don't have to let the listener know exactly what the lyrics mean. If you feel something specific when you write your lyrics and express those feelings with an original set of words, then you'll communicate the feeling when you sing it. Listeners have their own set of personal experiences they can apply to the words. (And please, no clichés! "Ooo babay, you durive me krazy" has no meaning for anyone unless the song title is "Tired Rock Phrases I Hope Never to Hear Again.")

Just like with the music, I have no rules for you to follow when writing lyrics. They don't have to rhyme, they don't have to "make sense," and they certainly don't have to follow rules of grammar. You should love them enough to sing them over and over again without embarrassment.

SPECIAL PROCESS FOR LYRICISTS

1. Promise the band after rehearsal that you'll write something for that awesome jam they came up with.

2. Watch some TV: *Matlock, Talk Soup, Batman*, etc. Listen to *Crooked Rain, Crooked Rain* and fall asleep.

3. Show up at next practice empty-handed and say, "I'm not into this one, it's not working for me."

4. Guitarist continues to play the damn riff.

5. Under duress—they're basically tapping their feet waiting for some vocalizing out of you—mumble some lyrics right there about how much you hate your band and would rather be watching another episode of *Matlock*.

6. Bassist mishears your mumblings and recites back what he thinks he heard: "Panty toilet dirty devil?! Genius!"

7. Accept the compliment graciously. Your genius knows no bounds.

Words from an Expert

This is what Tim says: *"I know if I read the lyrics and they don't say what I mean, then the song needs work. My song fails if its meaning gets lost; if I don't speak my mind clearly and I convolute my message. I can't just sing anything and nonsense; I'm not Michael Stipe. People might interpret the song's message differently, but I want to express it in a way that makes the meaning clear—to me.*

"A good song stands up to criticism. If I've worked hard and been careful about the structures and been honest, then the song will back itself up. It still hurts when people criticize your songs, but you can take it if your song says what you want.

"Even after all that, you know, a song might fail because it just does not rock. You have to be able to dance and move on stage to your own stuff."

Once the song hangs together loosely in jam form, only a sudden wave of forgetfulness will prevent you from arranging and finishing it. Believe it or not, unexpected memory loss has ruined many quality jams—every note! It happens like this: during a rehearsal session that produced some genius noises, you stop to go to the bathroom and then have some discussion about who will be driving to that Soundgarden show next weekend, so everyone gets sidetracked. You all forgot your parts, didn't you? It sounds like a ridiculous problem that only the stupidest musician would encounter, right? Uh, yeah. Well, in defense of stupid musicians, it's just that people relax a little too much during a great jam to think consciously about what exactly their fingers are doing. Use a tape recorder when you write, or take notes.

WRITING SONGS BY YOURSELF

You don't have to jam with your band all the time. Bits and pieces of songs will come like heavenly beams at unexpected moments, like when you watch TV, take a long bus ride, or study for finals. When you least expect it, your muse may visit; or you can sit down with only an instrument and your active head to write songs. Lots of bands have one member who "writes" all the songs: comes up with the idea and tells other band members what to play. Such a person usually has their shit together, musically, but not always.

SPECIAL PROCESS FOR WRITERS WITH A COMPLETE VISION

*L*ee plays no instruments, but writes the songs for his band alone—in a state of total musical ignorance:

"*E*ven before I started a band, I noticed that I was getting melodies in my head. (Granted, this was after taking a lot of psychedelic drugs and smoking pot every day.) Anyway, I would lay in bed in the morning or late at night, humming, and sometimes I would compose whole songs, with bass, guitar, vocals, drums, the whole thing. I realized that I could write songs because I could hear them in my head, but I don't know any music. I don't know a D chord from, like, anything. So I would run to the nearest piece of paper and try to put words to it, throwing any words to it that would remind me how the melody went in my head [note the panicky fear of memory loss]. Any stupid thing, even if it was 'the cat in the hat was black.' Then I got a tape recorder, so I'd run to the tape recorder when I got an idea so I'd have something to bring to practice and the other guys could hear it like that.

"Now, after four years, I don't need to rely on my notes or my tape recorder, but the best results happen when I can get it out of my head in the most recognizable way. I still don't know music but we all work together. My band knows how to deal with that by now."

Other songwriters have a more liberal method.

SPECIAL PROCESS FOR WRITERS WITH A COMPLETE VISION THAT THEY MAKE AVAILABLE FOR "INTERPRETATION" AND FUCKUP

In a way similar to Lee's method, the songwriter comes up with the melody, riff and other parts in her head. Then at rehearsal, the band does not convert those ideas into the noises she heard. Maybe they aren't paying attention, maybe they don't have the skills, maybe they have their own ideas. The song evolves. It's almost impossible to tell someone else what to play or sing if you can't play or sing it yourself. Your verbal instruction has different meaning to different people, and of course, inexperience limits a band's choices.

All this may frustrate the person whose idea you are trying to understand; and the band may become very irritated if they feel like someone is giving orders. Often the original idea has to be left behind because the band has moved in a different direction from that idea, using everyone's contribution to form a song that reflects your band's unique sound.

Phase II

Now that you have some parts, you can start to arrange the song. In this phase you will find places for all the bits and pieces so that the song has a specific structure and everyone knows what will happen next as they play. Don't worry that discipline and restraint will ruin the cool energy of your freestyling jam, because that energy happens when you play together. Nervousness during a live show or recording session could ruin the cool energy altogether, so having a plan to depend on will ease minds when the situation becomes stressful.

With the band: As you play, the song may just evolve from one part to a second part, and structure may emerge naturally. Or, someone with leadership qualities might assert some changes while you jam by hollering "go back to that first part," or "do that again" every so often, to give it basic structure. Eventually, though, you have to stop, sort the music out, and review your chaos.

First, figure out how many distinct parts you played and identify them. This may take awhile if everyone played all over the place at once. It doesn't matter how you identify the pieces—part A, part 1, "the noisy part," etc.—so long as everyone knows what's going on when you discuss them. As you gain experience trying to articulate details about notes and timing, the band will develop a weird, private language that no one else can understand. For now, however, expect confusion.

Ask each member to show the class what they were playing during each of the parts. They'll often surprise you by revealing something entirely different from what you thought you heard, or by having no idea what they played (see, that, um, whattayoucall—oh! memory loss again). Talk about which parts you love, which parts you hate, and which parts have "weirdness" about them. Try to be as specific as you can with your reactions. You may hate a particular part that the rest of the band loves, and if you cannot come up with a reason, they sometimes get mad or frustrated. Decide whether the "weird" noise you heard sounds good or bad; and if the badness came because the timing was off, someone played wack notes, or some other reason.

Play each part by itself awhile to get a feel for it outside of the song, then decide how long you want it to go when you play it in the song. Then play the different parts next to one another to see if they flow together in a pleasing way. Your band's new language will increase its vocabulary here, too, as you try to measure the parts. A band who doesn't know the proper terms for musical timing could simply say, "Let's do that sugary part twice as an intro, then the drums come in and we'll do it four times, then go to the Neil Young–esque part for twice as long as before." Listen to each other carefully, entertain every idea and suggestion; and as you throw things out and keep others, you will gradually pound the song into shape.

This organizing phase, called arranging, can really try your patience. Often the band tries to work out some idea and it just won't come together, or someone can't figure out what they want to play and says, "Can you guys just play those two notes over and over again until I come up with something?"

You might structure the song before you've created the parts to fill it: "Let's start out really loud, then drop down to just vocals, then sort of build back up again..." or, "Let's do a part where just the bass and drums go for a while and the lyrics come in sort of shouted..." With specific ideas like those, you can keep a goal in mind when you jam.

Alone: Arranging your own song is like grading your own exam—it all sounds good to you. Without other musicians as your sounding board, you can freely arrange everything the way you think it should go. Use a tape recorder to experiment with various ideas. Record your main part, or the one that's most prominent in your head. Then as you play it back, you can create complementary parts. Just like you would with the band, label the parts somehow and put them together. A four-track tape deck can help you organize your ideas and construct songs by yourself.

Again, sudden memory loss may trouble you, and it's worse when you're alone. Walking home from a friend's house, for example, you find that her copy of a classic Flaming Lips album has inspired you with a musical vision. You create a rhythm, pair it with a few choice phrases, imagine a bass part, then a guitar part, a guitar solo, and a really cool ending. If the phone rings as you walk in the door or your roommate asks whether you paid the rent—whoosh!—your masterpiece has vanished. The only cure for this is to call your answering machine and sing it to yourself in a message, or run for the closest piece of paper to take notes.

Don't expect the most enthusiastic reception of your masterpiece at the next rehearsal when you play your tapes and try to communicate your genius to the band. These little taped ideas often don't sound so thrilling to anyone but their creator. If your bandmates narrow their eyes or laugh and don't want to help you iron the whole thing out, save the idea for your solo album.

After you've brought your song through those two phases, it has an arrangement, and everyone knows his part, you'll probably decide it's finished. Don't high-five each other and book time at the recording studio just yet. Even if the whole thing seems to have structure, you still have to play the song together about a hundred times to tighten it up. Each time you do, you'll hear things that you think could be better, you'll play with more precision, and you'll see the song as a more complete work. Some songs never stop changing in small ways and getting better each time they're played. When you play live (eventually), the song will grow then too, and come together in another different way.

SONGWRITING RUTS

"Same boring stuff again tonight?" Hopefully you don't encounter a songwriter's block this early in your career, but sometimes things get a bit stuck. Don't let flabby rhythms and stale riffs sour your mood. Work a new way; here's how:

- Ask someone who doesn't usually make the first move to come up with an idea, especially the drummer.

- Bring your own ideas in, even if they're incomplete.

- The problem could be your record collection. Too much Bush and you'll never spawn another original idea.

- Borrow tapes and CDs from other people.

- Have band members make tapes of music featuring cool examples of your instrument.

- Listen to music you ordinarily wouldn't and try to pick out aspects of it that you would like to hear in your own music.

- Take lessons. Learning a few new tricks never hurt.

- Write a lot. Make ten OK songs or ten half-assed ideas into three really great songs.

- Regiment yourself and write all the time, even when you're drunk or sad or sleepy.

Perhaps the problems you have go deeper. Does the songwriting process bruise your ego? Your band won't listen to you or would rather bicker than play music? You will see clashes and power struggles when you write songs, even in the most harmonious bands.

What are you talking about? First, let your band know why you're unhappy. They love you and want to help, so discuss these things calmly with them. Don't forget that none of you really knows how to communicate musical ideas, so misunderstandings will happen all the time. Be sure you know what someone means before you let their words upset you.

Keep an open mind. Band members might bring in suggestions that you can't stand. Keep your mouth shut until you hear the idea for yourself. A dumb idea might sound great when played, or might sound great after you ruin it the right way. More important, a person who doesn't feel their ideas are given any weight will resent the rest of you, and that's the start of bad feelings in the band. Respect your band members, and if you really hate everything that one of them comes up with, even after you complete a song together, maybe they (or you) should not stay in the band.

Be fair to new ideas. Is it the new idea that bothers you or something else? Try to understand where your bad feelings come from. Does that new idea your drummer suggested require more work for you? Do you have to change something you really like? Did she present it in a way that insulted you? Had you hoped for something different? These are things to talk about as you write songs together, and you have to be honest with yourself when you react.

What's your problem? Maybe you feel lazy, maybe you're in a bad mood, maybe you just think it sucks and you can't explain why. Ask yourself before you shout down someone else's attempts to make a song better. You cannot write good songs in an atmosphere where someone feels uncomfortable about expressing himself. Everyone should have a say.

The last thing to remember about writing songs: don't take it seriously and don't stress. No set of rules dictates that noise should have certain characteristics before it earns the title "Song." So what if your composition is silly or dumb or too short or too long? You're allowed to do whatever you want. You are the artist. You cannot be stopped.

5

WELCOME TO THE

RUSTY SCUPPER

(Your Live Performance)

NECESSARY MATERIALS:
> Instruments—yours and anyone else's you can get your hands on.
> Songs to play and a set list so you know when to play them.
> Earplugs—those other bands might really suck.
> Extra 9-volt batteries, picks, sticks, strings, and cables.
> A pen in case you meet anyone interesting after the show.

ATTITUDE: As much as you can muster.

FILTH FACTOR: There's a reason why nightclubs are so dark inside.

DANGEROUSNESS: Well, let's see: you'll be in some seedy club, late at night, with a pile of expensive equipment and perhaps a small wad of cash. I'd say the situation could be a bit dicey.

OPPORTUNITIES FOR ROMANCE: Many—if anyone comes to the show.

MUSICAL IMPORTANCE: Major.

76

PRICE: You may actually earn a little money.

TIME: All night, from 5:00 P.M. until about 1:00 A.M. or later.

POTENTIAL FOR HUMILIATION: Imagine yourself on stage singing and playing a loud instrument very badly while other people sit at the bar and try to enjoy a baseball game on TV. Never mind the Braves, pay attention to the band!

ou will quickly discover that making noise in a basement does not resemble a real gig. As you write and rehearse your songs down there next to a pile of laundry and a table saw, your imagination can go crazy—the adoring throng, the guest appearance on MTV's *House of Style*, the big tour plans ("They're gonna love us in Japan"); and you may think you have a pretty accurate idea of how being on stage will feel. Just wait. Like sex, your first time will frighten and embarrass you just as much as it excites you—oh, and it's really really fun.

Playing in front of an audience is a major first step for a band. Even though you have been writing and practicing together, things happen at a live show that nothing can prepare you for: equipment problems, nervousness, a hostile crowd (or no crowd at all), a dark stage with blazing red and yellow lights. You don't rehearse under these conditions, so you cannot predict how they will affect your performance. All you will have to fall back on are your songs.

The most important component for a successful live show is a great set of songs. (Yes, amps and instruments are handy, but you can borrow all of that stuff for now.) For a party or another relaxed kind of situation where you'll play in front of friends, five or six songs is enough to make an appearance. A standard set lasts about forty minutes, though, so make sure you have at least twenty-five to thirty minutes of music and clever banter ready when you book a show at a real club—that's about nine songs. Keep an eye on the clock at rehearsal; maybe your six songs each take five minutes to play.

Six great songs makes a stronger set than nine crappy ones, so use the music to measure your readiness, not the amount of time it takes to play your set. Make a tape of your set and pretend to be in the audience when you listen to it. Ask yourself: Are these songs good? Is this band good? Was it worth it to drive out here and pay the cover charge? Am I having fun or do I feel like stepping out to 7-Eleven for a large cup of coffee and a set of earplugs? Once you have a decent set of music ready for other people to hear, book a show right away. Of course, you could wait until the songs are tighter or until your band improves to play out, but now you're making excuses. Just get your butts on stage and play; live performances will make your band better faster than any basement exercises.

Problem is, you have to convince someone that you can play a good show in order to get a booking. This may present a challenge since you've never played out. I can suggest no tricks, but I do know of three ways to get a show.

1. PLAY A PARTY

At a party, you can set up your own situation and get those special on-stage feelings without dealing with a club. When you hear about some out-of-control house party, art gallery opening, or school event, ask the party-thrower if you can entertain the guests with some live music. Set up early in the evening and do a set before the place gets crowded, just to see how things go and to check your sound. If disaster strikes, you have options (such as leaving immediately); if you avoid disaster, then play a second set after everyone shows up. The crowd will forgive any problems because they haven't paid to see a "concert," and afterward you can mingle and possibly enjoy free beverages. Unfortunately, you'll probably have to bring all your own equipment, including PA or an amp for the vocals—I'll talk about that in a couple of pages.

2. HOOK UP

If the social calendar looks bleak, hook up with another band and open for them. You may need to ingratiate yourselves a bit, but latching onto another band is the best way to get a show and this method offers lots of good opportunities. Choose a sympathetic band and ask if they have any no-big-deal shows coming up and can you please open up for them. Clubs often ask their headlining band for suggestions to fill the other time slots, so don't be shy. Your offer may help them out. Playing at a club for the first time by the good graces of another band gives you an important chance to meet the club's booker and establish a relationship with her.

3. THE HARD WAY

Lisa White books shows at the 9:30 Club in Washington, D.C., and she has excellent advice for bands who want first-time bookings.

Call the club and find out the name of the person who books shows. Get the correct spelling of their name, their address and phone number (sometimes the booker doesn't work at the club), and ask what days of the week or hours of the day are best to call. Then, send a package to the booker that includes a tape of your band and a note. Band photos, articles in newspapers or fanzines and the occasional bribe are OK too, but only the tape and the note are really necessary, Lisa says.

The items in your package may get strewn all over someone's desk after it's opened, so make sure each piece has the band's name and a contact phone number on it. Only one contact per band, please. The booker doesn't want to talk to everyone, just the person with the most business sense and verbal technique. Write a short note with information that lets her know you are serious and have your shit together.

Put all these things in a padded envelope. "Nothing fancy or expensive," Lisa recommends, "but definitely make it look nice and stand out." She waves toward a huge, wheeled cart in her office piled high with this week's mail—hundreds of brown or yellow padded envelopes that all look exactly alike. "If it looks special, even if there's something cool inside, like a rubber alligator or something [cheapie bribe or gimmicky doo-dad], then I'll remember it. One band even cut up a potato and made a print all over the outside of the envelope."

Follow up with a phone call. Bigger clubs need four to six weeks to listen to all the tapes they get. Check up on a smaller place in about two to three weeks. Ask the booker if she listened to your tape. If she says no, find out when you can call her again. If she says yes, she will probably also say she liked it and wants to book your band, or didn't like it—and no thanks. Don't get all upset and defensive on the phone when you hear bad news. People who book clubs hear hundreds and hundreds of tapes each month. They're pretty objective and they can suggest changes that might make your band better. Besides, you want to make friends with bookers across the land, so find out what turned this one off to your tape. The most common problem, Lisa says, is that "the band sounds like stuff everyone's heard before, especially Pearl Jam and R.E.M." (ouch); or that "the tape just sucks; poor quality, can't hear anything."

FIG. 11. THE PACKAGE FOR CLUB BOOKERS

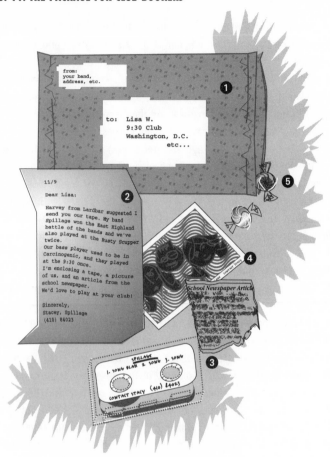

1. Eye-Catching Package
   In a padded envelope with groovy decoration; complete address and correct spelling of the booker's name.
2. Letter
   A little name-dropping gets their attention. Include band credentials and important achievements and list the envelope's contents. Sign off with one contact name and number.
3. Tape
   Labeled with song titles, contact name and phone number.
4. Photo and Press
   Not necessary, but write your name on it if you do send one.
5. Cheapie Bribe
   Also not necessary, but often works. In this case a couple of mint candies left over from a trip to Pizza Hut.

No one wants to hear that their masterpieces sound sucky, but don't take it too hard. Lisa really means that you have a lot of work to do, and since you're a beginner you knew that already. Ask her if she has any specific suggestions and while you ponder her advice, send your tape to other clubs.

Don't worry that you won't be able to get shows when your town's Lisa says, "Thanks but no thanks." Once word gets out that you've gotten a band together and are seriously rehearsing, people in other bands or show organizers will ask you to play, and you will eventually be able to get on the bill at the coolest places.

When someone asks you to play a show, make sure you get all the information you need from the booker or whomever you have on the phone; they call it *advancing the show*. Ask as many questions as you can think of when you make the arrangements, and if you book with someone from another band who answers "I don't know" or "I guess," then get a contact at the club and ask someone who knows. See Figure 12 for details.

You can make the show go easier by sharing equipment with the other bands on the bill. If you cannot rely on your own gear, if your small car won't hold everything, or if the other band have just been shopping with the advance from their record company, ask the booker for some phone numbers so that you can wheel and deal—your band may have equipment that others want to use as well. Borrowing may not solve any problems, though, if the other band doesn't show up at all, doesn't want to stay until your 1:00 A.M. set, or actually has equipment crappier than yours. In the event of an equipment emergency, ask the booker or sound person for help. They've done all this before. The very worst circumstances may force you to rent from the local guitar shop, but you should only do that in the most dire situation.

Stay in contact with the club after you book the show. Call a couple of days in advance to reconfirm the show and sound check times. Get the number of the sound person and find out what he needs from you, and describe your setup and instruments. If you've played live before, describe anything that gave you problems or worked out well.

FIG. 12

ADVANCING THE SHOW

Venue_____   Show Date_____

Address_____   Lineup_____

Phone_____   _____

Booker_____   _____

Sound Person_____   _____

Sound Check Time_____   _____

Will we get paid?   y   n

Does the place have a PA?   y   n

Do they serve alcohol?   y   n

Do our friends need id's to get in?   y   n

**Tell the booker about underage
band members?**   y   n

**Can we share equipment with the
other bands?**   y   n

Get their phone numbers_____

How many guests do we get?_____

Where do we load in?_____

Anything else?_____

The Big Night Arrives!

Pack everything you might possibly need into the car or van. Don't let another band member pack your stuff because they always space out and leave something behind ("Uh, I forgot those thingies"). Along with all the usual gear, bring extra sticks, picks, cables, and strings. Drive safely, now, and get there on time. Drag your stuff inside, say hello, and figure out who's who: the booker you spoke to on the phone, the sound person, etc. Make friends, and let the people who run the joint know that this will be your first time on stage. Ask the sound person if you will still be getting a sound check (often they promise at the outset but can't deliver).

This *Will* Happen to You

You arrive at the Rusty Scupper, eager (and maybe a little nervous) to play your first live show—yay. Hmmm, no one is there. Doors are locked, parking lot's empty. You check your calendar, call the club (maybe they can't hear you pounding on the door)—nothing. So you slump down near the door and try to remain calm. Another band shows up. They don't seem worried: "Oh, yeah, this guy's never on time," they say, and head off to their drummer's girlfriend's house. One hour later, the manager shows up and unlocks the doors. You go in and set up your gear, but the sound person still hasn't arrived, and neither has the headlining band. Wait, here he is! And the other band ("Now we're rolling," you think.) The headlining band sets up their equipment, but only after chatting with the club owner, smoking a few cigarettes, making a phone call, and unpacking their gear. They run through a few songs, but the other band's not back from wherever. "Dudes, we're running a little late," says the sound guy. "If they don't show up within the next ten minutes, you can't check—gotta open the doors in a half hour." Uh, OK.

SOUND CHECK

The band that goes on first—probably yours—will sound check last and then just leave the stuff on stage. Headliners or later bands will check their sound first and then put their stuff away. When the club has a proper sound system, they hire someone to run it—the sound person. The purpose of a sound check is for the sound person to learn what levels sound best for each instrument and for the band as a whole, and then to use those levels during your set. Sounds easy, right?

Robin Danar knows a lot about sound. He has worked at clubs and arenas of all sizes and has produced records too. His job, as he describes it, is to "take what's already there and fill the room with it." Notice that he didn't mention taking a shitty set of noises and making them orchestral, or taking your out-of-tune, clunky songs and creating masterpieces. "Shit in, shit out," he explains, correctly represents the process of sound work (in vulgar rock language) when there isn't much to work with. "I can't make your band better—that's your job. I'm there to reinforce your sound and make it balanced."

Your goal: sound great on stage. Robin's goal: create a house mix that sounds comparable to the stage sound, but hyped.

For a successful sound check, he first suggests that you get to the club about a half hour before your sound check and set up the drums off stage, so that everything's ready to just lift up there when your turn comes. Anything you do to speed up the process works in your favor, because the doors are going to open whether you've had a sound check or not.

Figure out where on the stage you want to be and put your amps behind you in a sort of horseshoe formation so that you can hear it. The sound guy will be on stage with you to help you place things in the right positions. He may hoist smaller amps up onto chairs or milk crates to better project their sound. He may suggest that you switch positions. Then, while the band prepares to play just as you would in rehearsal—looking for outlets, untangling your cords and adjusting your cymbals—he will place microphones and direct boxes and other sound things in front of or on top of your equipment. He will place microphones for the vocalists, he will unwind lots of cables. You just set up and get ready to play.

Get your sound as perfect as possible while the sound person works on stage with you. Leave your settings at the levels you use during rehearsal, adjust your pedals, check your cables, and tune your guitars. Tell him when you're ready. He'll go across the room to the mixing board, and use a microphone to speak to you. He will listen to each instrument separately and then listen to you as you play together.

First, the drums. When he says, "Can I hear the bass drum," everyone should stop making noise. The drummer goes *boom boom boom* until told, "That's enough." "Can I hear the snare?" The drummer goes bap, bap, bap . . . You get the idea. Just follow his instructions. Bass often comes next, then guitars, and vocals anywhere in there. Don't get goofy or embarrassed when it comes your turn, just give steady, repetitive tones so that he can adjust his levels, and play like you normally do, no harder or softer.

After getting the individual instrument levels, you'll do a song from your set together. Choose one with lots of variation, so that the sound guy can hear each instrument. "Something spatial," Robin suggests, "and not too loud." Listen carefully as you play this song. Make sure that you can hear everything and that you sound like you want to sound. The band will sound different on stage than at rehearsal, but you shouldn't sound that different, warns Robin, even if you're playing someone else's equipment. All the noises come from your instruments or your mouth. You control them, so pay careful attention during sound check and communicate with the sound person. Speak up right away if you can't hear something or have some other problem, make any adjustments you need, then do part of your set's first song. If everything sounds OK (and sometimes even if it doesn't), sound check ends. Remember where you've set all your levels and get your stuff offstage right away (unless you're the opening band) so that the next band can sound check, or the club can open. Now, you probably have some time to waste. Put your equipment in the back room or wherever everyone else has put theirs, write down your guest list and give it to the door person, and go find some food.

You may not get a sound check. If no sound check happens, just make sure you sound as together as possible before you start. Singers should sing into the mikes as the other instruments set up. The sound person will quickly check the mikes and monitors. Everyone turn the volume down just a notch lower than usual and open your set with a song that has an extended intro; this allows the sound person an opportunity to make adjustments, if possible, early on. Then, after the first song, make adjustments on stage and tell the sound person if you can't hear something.

Attitude Alert! Sound Guys

Yeah, a lot of the time they're unfriendly or don't listen to what you want. But that job is no picnic. The work starts at 7:00 P.M. and doesn't finish until 3:00 A.M., wrangling five or more bands on stage, getting their levels, dealing with their problems, then hurrying them off stage in a timely manner. Cigarette smoke, noise, and booze make for a pretty abusive atmosphere, and the pay sucks—$50 or less for the night. Insurance? Benefits? Paid vacation? Please.

Just remember: a grouchy sound person could ruin your evening with the flick of the wrist, or his extra effort could make you sound great, so put on your sweetest face and always say please.

THE SOUND SYSTEM

Understanding the sound person's tools and how the system works will give you more control over your show. When you play live, there are two ways that the audience might hear your sound. First, they could all be sitting cross-legged on a Persian rug listening intently like the audience does during a poetry reading, and the sound would be coming directly from the guitar, pure and undistorted. Nice, maybe, but the second and more fun way is to use modern technology and play very loud.

On stage, the sound person sets up microphones for singers and in front of most instruments. Cables connect these microphones to inputs on the mixing board. Some instruments sound better when their signal goes directly to the board, bypassing the microphone. To satisfy a feedback lover, or to get a greater variety of sounds, Robin might set up a microphone *and* a direct box and bring two separate signals from the instrument and blend them together at the mixing board.

Microphones will also bring drum sounds into the audience. The bass drum almost always has a microphone—it goes right inside that little hole on the front. And another mike brings out the sounds of the snare and hi-hat. Bigger places with more extensive systems and higher-paid sound reinforcement staff will obviously have a more complex system to create killer sounds for the audience.

Back at the mixing board, each microphone or direct line comes into its own channel, or input, on the board. A fader determines the level and a bunch of knobs control the tone. Robin makes a mix for the audience to hear and sends that to the speakers above the band's head or in front of the stage. Usually the band won't hear this mix very well, but will hear the auxiliary mixes that go to the monitors sitting on stage pointed at your heads.

OK, so everyone in the room will hear something slightly different. Up on stage you will hear the live sounds coming from your amps and from the drums, in combination with the noises coming from the monitors. The audience members up front near the stage will hear the band's live sounds combined with the mix that the sound person sends to the speakers, and they may hear some of the noises coming out of the monitors. Robin will only hear his house mix coming from the speakers and maybe some of the noises from the stage if the sound board is close enough. Audience members at the bar will mostly hear the house

FIG. 13. THE SOUND SYSTEM

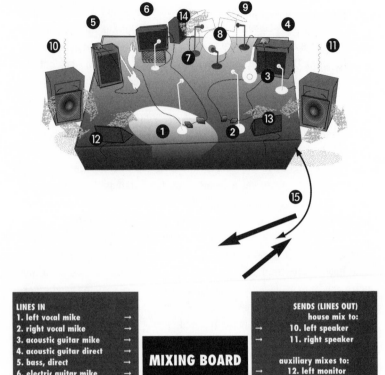

LINES IN		
1. left vocal mike	→	
2. right vocal mike	→	
3. acoustic guitar mike	→	
4. acoustic guitar direct	→	
5. bass, direct	→	
6. electric guitar mike	→	
7. snare mike	→	
8. bass drum mike	→	
9. hi-hat mike	→	

MIXING BOARD

SENDS (LINES OUT)	
house mix to:	
→	10. left speaker
→	11. right speaker
auxiliary mixes to:	
→	12. left monitor
→	13. right monitor
→	14. drum monitor

This basic schematic shows how a regular club with a sound system might set it up. Each place, of course, sets its system up differently, and your band might not have the same elements as this imaginary band. But this diagram should give you the general idea.

Microphones send the vocals (1, 2), drum sounds (7,8,9), and guitar sounds (3, 6) from the stage directly to the board. Direct boxes send bass signals (5) and acoustic guitar signals (4) to the board. (Effects pedals work the same whether the instrument's sound goes direct or through a mike.) Check out what the clever sound person did with the acoustic guitar: a direct box and microphone. The sound person creates a mix for the audience and sends it to the speakers (10, 11) while auxiliary mixes bring different mixes of the band's sounds to the monitors on stage (12, 13, 14) so that they can hear themselves and each other. The snake (15) contains all the cables going to and coming from the stage; look for it along the club's ceiling.

mix. Also, people standing in different areas, both on stage and in the audience, will hear slightly different mixes. It's all very wacky.

So what's the point of a sound check if you aren't hearing what it will really sound like? Um, good point, but you *are* hearing what it will really sound like to you, and since your goal is to sound good on stage and play well, you hear what you need to hear. Also, since the sound person is hearing what it will sound like in the audience, he's hearing everything that he needs to hear. You certainly are welcome to step off stage into the room during sound check to hear the levels.

Unfortunately, all of the above simply represents the theoretical sound situation. Tons of sonic eccentricities will thwart you. When you first begin to play out, bad sound will confuse you on stage; but after a number of shows you'll learn to play well in spite of having no vocals in your monitor or hearing nothing but bass. You simply have no control over the sound system or the sound person, so try to make sure you *can* hear what you need to hear (and that you like the quality of the sound). After that, have faith in your sound person and accept the fact that even with his seasoned expertise and a thorough sound check, your first two or three songs often won't sound quite right.

UP THERE

"Hey, Lemonade Vision," says the sound person, "get up there." (If you're not first in the lineup, start dragging your equipment on stage as soon as the band before you gets most of theirs off.) Uh, OK, your big moment has arrived. Too bad the place is completely deserted because it's only 8:00. If you think that your friends really will come to see you, beg the dude to wait fifteen minutes till at least one or two of them show up. Then get your butts on stage and check your levels to see that they haven't been bumped awry as you dragged your stuff on and off. Look at your bandmates to make sure everyone's ready—no giggling, now—and play your songs! Pay close attention to the sound during the first few songs, even if you've had a sound check. If you start playing and find you can't hear something or someone's real loud, step up to the mike and politely ask the sound person about it. During the show, do not mess with the positions of the microphones next to your equipment.

HOW DO YOU LOOK?

Don't worry about that now. Sure, it's nice to glance up from your instrument once in awhile or to actually move around on stage, but I suggest that you just concentrate on putting your fingers and feet where they have to go for the first couple of shows and save the antics for when you know your songs inside and out. Musicians who have been playing for years and have been on stage hundreds of times can dangle from the rafters and make mental grocery lists while they play flawless sets, but you ain't all that yet. Keep an eye on your band to make sure no catastrophes have occurred over at the other end of the stage and to give the impression that you all at least know one another. And when your friends complain that your show was boring to watch, tell them that it's meant to be an audio experience for now.

NERVOUS?

Until your big debut, you cannot estimate whether you'll be nervous, or if nervousness will affect your performance. Look for serious anxiety during sound check, because that's when everything starts to feel very real and very much out of your control. "Oh-my-god! I'm on the stage of this club and soon I will play my little songs in front of all these people. I feel faint." Watch for these other ugly symptoms of stage fright: playing every song at twice its tempo; inability to recognize your instrument or any of its components; continuing to play after the song is over; confusion about how the next song starts, how your part goes, how your part after that goes, how many times you play it, how it ends; playing the entire song out of tune; looking over at your bandmates and feeling like they are far, far away, even on the tiniest stage; not looking up again at all after that.

BEWARE THE LIGHTS!

When they're off, you can't see your fingers but you can see the stunned, silent faces in the audience. When they're on, you can see your fingers but you might momentarily blind yourself with a careless glance toward the ceiling. And they heat you up. The orange bulbs that make you sweat buckets on stage are the same ones that keep hot dogs warm and sweaty in the Woolworth's cafeteria—I think.

You've given oral presentations, you've run races, and you've been called on to share the joke with the rest of the class, so you know about performance anxiety. Do whatever you need to ease your fear. Pace around, hide backstage, go to the bathroom, chew your fingernails off. Make your set list into a cheat sheet, with reminders about the first note or word of the song, or equipment adjustments. Tune your guitar in the back room and run through the set in your head.

If you really can't relax, medicate yourself with a minimal amount of alcohol or nicotine (unless prohibited by law, of course), and comfort yourself with the fact that it will all be over in less than a half hour.

AFTER

If the audience doesn't clamor for encores, say goodnight. Relieved and excited? You may not party yet. Pack up your toys and slide them out of the way or backstage. Do not put your stuff in the car/van until you're ready to leave. Your sorry, rusted-out van full of musical equipment is just too easy a target for thieves. Help yourself to a (hopefully complimentary) beverage at the bar but remember all that drunk-driving stuff they teach you at school—get home safely.

Then, when it's time to go, locate the booker or doorperson and find out if you earned any money, take a peek at the guest list to see which of your deadbeat friends didn't show up even though you comped them, and thank everybody. Oh, and many self-pats on the back.

Please Play Safely

Remember that one kid at camp whose mother sewed her darling's name into every piece of clothing? You are now that woman. Equipment disappears all the time—and appears all the time: "Whose tuner is this in my bag?" I don't mean to get all nerdy with you now, but you gotta write your name on all your stuff. Or else when some dork from Back in Black, Jersey's finest AC/DC cover band, finds your distortion pedal in the trunk of his car, it'll never return to you. Some other things you must not do:

- Don't ever leave anything in the van, especially in the club's parking lot.

- Don't leave your guitars at the club after sound check if you get a creepy vibe there.

- Don't wander around a strange neighborhood by yourselves at night—get directions from club staff.

- Don't drink a bunch of beers and then drive home.

Huh?

We've become a nation of pussies. First we decided that getting tanked and driving home is no longer acceptable; then we started wearing seat belts; after that we changed our minds about smoking and outlawed it in public buildings; and finally, we let earplugs infringe on rock's essential, self-destructive machismo!

Yes, OK, I'm being facetious, but only because I care. Loud noises cause pain and irreparable damage to your ears, whether they come from a lawn mower, a shotgun, or a Marshall stack. You've seen those pictures of the inner ear's delicate structure—sound wave vibrations go all over inside there and can damage all that stuff, but one of the parts is particularly vulnerable. The cochlea (from the italian word for snail, get it?), this spiraling tube inside your head, does most of the hearing. The cochlea's inner walls sprout these microscopic clusters of hairy-looking cells that vibrate when sounds hit them, and send information about the vibrations through the auditory nerve to the brain, and you know what goes on in there. ("Yo, my favorite tune.") Those microscopic sprouts suffer crucial damage when you expose them to high volumes.

Here's what happens: J Mascis turns on his amp and begins to play at a volume way over 95 dB—that's the low end of harmful levels—and probably hits 115 dB or more during the more thrilling parts of his show. Those little sprouts in the ear lie down like palm trees in a hurricane of high-frequency and high volume. They can't take it. (If you take a break from the show, even for just ten or fifteen minutes, you give those sprouts an opportunity to rest and repair themselves.) After the show, you and your friends go to Denny's, where your hollering frightens other diners. YOU'VE SUFFERED THRESHOLD SHIFT and you can't hear things at their normal volume! Later that night the ringing in your ears keeps you awake, and the next day your hearing is fine because those little cells do recover after a brief episode.

What about J's ears? If Mascis can still hear, it's because he has protected his ears. Those sprouts tend to recover less and less with repeated exposure, until they don't recover at all. How many concerts before you go deaf? What row do you have to stand in? Do Marshall amps cause more damage than Peaveys? Unfortunately, human knowledge does not extend that far. We do know, however, that high frequencies hurt your ears before low frequencies do. If you were to turn up the bass amp until it hurt your ears then do the same with the guitar amp, and measure the decibel level coming from each, you'd find the bass volume to be much higher. During a live performance, however, those high frequencies don't just come from the guitars; the vocals, drums and even the bass create a barrage of damaging noises.

Tinnitus, a high-pitched ringing or whistling sound, is a symptom of overexposure that you hear in your head. Many ear afflictions cause tinnitus, just like many head afflictions cause headaches, but the tinnitus resulting from noise-induced hearing loss is permanent. It interferes with listening, writing music, and playing, and it could finish your musical endeavors before old age does.

So, wear earplugs and wear them often. Different kinds of earplugs do different things. Some just indiscriminately block out high frequencies—great for jackhammer operators but bad for musicians. You'll miss the guitars, some of the vocals, and who knows what else. Audiologists have invented acoustically friendly earplugs that allow you to experience a lower-decibel level of all the music's frequencies. Problem is, they're expensive and must be custom made to fit your ear. Cheaper types from the drugstore don't reduce the noises evenly or fit as well, but they help. Check for a noise reduction rating on the package to make sure they aren't for swimming or something.

It does not matter which kind you choose, just make sure you have a pair on hand so that whenever you plan to encounter live music you protect your hearing.

6

LET EVERYBODY
KNOW

(Promoting Your Show)

NECESSARY MATERIALS:
> A confirmed gig.
> A few good visual ideas.
> (Different methods require different supplies. See the recipes.)

ATTITUDE: That of stealthy urban terrorist *or* smiling office drone.

FILTH FACTOR: The highest.

DANGEROUSNESS: Oh, yes.

OPPORTUNITIES FOR ROMANCE: A few.

MUSICAL IMPORTANCE: Absolutely none.

PRICE: Sliding scale, but the best promotion is the cheapest.

TIME: Inversely proportional to money.

orry, but we have to talk about economics now. A bar or club makes money when people pay admission or buy drinks or both. More people equals more money. Your band's ability to attract a bunch of paying customers shows club owners that you are worthy of inviting back. Think about it. They have to pay a bartender and a doorperson and a sound person and pay their rent and electricity bills and blah blah. This ain't no charity! When you earn money for the club, the booker will want you to play at her club again. When you do not draw very many people, then it *is* charity and your band can't be choosy about future time slots or money or anything. So, get all your friends down there to see you play those lousy Monday evening shows, prove yourself, and next time you might play on a happening weekend night, and eventually you may earn opening slots for the coolest shows.

Unfortunately, a new band's first bunches of shows tend to suck as everyone learns to work their instruments and gets used to playing together in front of an audience. Your friends and family will think it's pretty entertaining to see you and your pals up on stage, but the novelty wears off pretty quick. Only the people whose unconditional love you enjoy—extremely faithful friends and family members—will attend every single show, but you have to try and pack the house each time, so invite every person you can possibly think of.

Even people you wouldn't normally invite anywhere make good audience members: your aunt and uncle, your lab partner, the girl whose feelings you hurt by not asking her to play guitar in the band (uh, maybe not). Take advantage of everyone's initial curiosity about your new project to fill the place. If your parents' friends or your psych professor want to see you play guitar and use four-letter words in a beer-splattered bar, invite them and respond happily if they come down to see you.

orry

But what if a million people come down and we suck?

Those million individuals know it's your first or second show, and they probably don't expect an orchestral sensation. Also, I can't think of a nice way to say it, but some aspects of your first live shows will absolutely, definitely be dreadful. Don't let that scare you. It doesn't mean you can't have fun on stage and put on a great show. You just started doing this about two chapters ago and it takes years to become a pro. Even genius, years-accomplished, cool-as-fuck musicians walk off stage thinking their show was awful sometimes. Sucking is totally irrelevant and often amusing.

Get ready for no-shows, too. Good intentions often fall far short of good deeds; it's the flaky nature of our species. The faces you most want to see in the audience often don't appear. Your best friend, who enthusiastically writes down the date of your next show on her calendar with, like, little stars around it or something, might never show up. Try not to get angry—in fact, get used to it. People don't realize how much effort a band requires or how much your band means to you; and a lot of people really don't enjoy live music, or perhaps they simply don't give a shit. For some of the people in your life, attending your little rock show is about as interesting as going to one of your third grade arts and crafts exhibits—yawn. "I'll go to the next one," they tell themselves.

Anyway, professionals have devised helpful methods of spreading the word about your show. Do these things and folks will come. Put on a good show and they will come back.

BY MOUTH

The telephone is your best tool for getting anything done. Didn't all your friends hear about your band within a week of its formation? Use the same expedient phone work to let them know about your shows. Go though your phone book and call everyone during the week before your gig. If you have tons of friends to call, do it during the day when answering machines cut down on the chitchat. Leave all the pertinent facts about the gig: date, time, place, and how much it costs. Then, tell them it will be fun and ask them to please bring other people. Inviting a friend to your show is not the same as borrowing their American history notes. Audience members aren't doing you a favor by coming to see your band, so do not make your performance sound like a chore or a test of friendship. People attend live musical events to drink drinks, enjoy music, hang out, and have fun; that's why they will be at your show. Don't sell yourself short.

BY MAIL

*E*veryone likes to find something odd in their mailbox, especially if it doesn't say CR-RT SORT at the top. A mailing list lets you get people's attention, gives you the chance to show what fascinating, creative individuals you are, and provides a way to invite people that you don't know or don't feel like talking to on the phone. To do a mailer you'll need names and addresses; you need invitations to send. See the recipe card.

Postcards go the cheapest, and letter-sized invitations are also pretty cheap, especially if someone in the band doubles as an office slave and can photocopy or use the postage meter for free. With unlimited resources, of course, you can send anything to folks on your mailing list. Make it clever and get their rapt attention.

Drop these things in the mail at least one week before the show. Sometimes they arrive overnight, but often your invitations are subject to the eccentricities of the United States Postal Service.

A mailing list requires more organization and costs more than most other forms of advertising, so you might not want to mail invitations for the first couple of shows, but you can start collecting names and addresses in a little notebook right away and then do a mailer when you have accumulated a bunch. Use a database or mailmerge program on the computer, if you can, that stores the information and allows you to print out mailing labels. Note the date that you get each address— especially for college students, who move pretty often—so that later you can knock people off the list who never come to see you.

FIG. 14. POSTCARDS

```
                    Postcards
Ingredients:
   * A letter-size sheet of paper, divided into quarters.
   * Some design.
   * Correct information about the show.

        It costs more to photocopy both sides of anything, so put all the
   information on one side and leave the reverse blank to stick on the
   address and stamp.
        Design four postcards, each with all the information. Ask the pho-
   tocopy place to print them onto cardstock and to cut them for you.
        Affix postage, affix or write addresses, and mail them out at
   least one week in advance.
```

(your original)   (your postcards)

A Trip to the Post Office

While the post office is a fun place to flip through mug shots looking for new boyfriends, doing anything else there can be a drag. Fortunately you can enjoy a mutually impersonal relationship with the post office that rivals the one you have with your bank.

First, prepare the mail according to United States Post Office standards. These standards usually involve (ominously enough) the threat of mail mutilation. Don't print your postcards on regular-weight paper because they could get mutilated; print them on cardstock, and cut them somewhere between the dimensions of 3½ by 5 inches and 4½ by 6 inches. Letters have to be less than one quarter inch thick; their length divided by height has to fall between 1.3 and 2.5; and they must weigh 1 ounce or less to avoid additional postage. They don't need an envelope, but your letter will better withstand the forces of mutilation from inside an envelope. Use padded envelopes or corrugated cardboard mailers for tapes, CDs, or singles. The ones with bubble-wrap inside are lighter-weight (and therefore cheaper to mail) than the paper-filled kind, but alas, they're non-recyclable. Use Jiffy #2's for singles and tapes—boost them from work or buy bulk. Seal all packages with real tape. The helpful postal service workers are supposed to tell you how best to pack any piece of mail, and if you don't follow their instructions (service with a snarl), again, you risk the mutilation or untimely return of your parcel. You can do all this at home, and if you can figure out how much the thing weighs (go to the grocery store), you can calculate the correct postage and mail it from home.

Stamps by mail! With this delightful system you avoid the hazards and hassles of a downtown visit. They accept checks and the stamps come pronto. Perfect for mailing lists.

First-class mail, which is how all letters and postcards travel, generally arrives at its destination within 1 to 3 days. Take your chances.

Any "indecent" language on the outside of the piece of mail could get you into trouble, and anything inside the mail that is obscene—"sexually arousing or explicit"—could also get you into trouble. Worse, if your mail exceeds the size limitations or your package doesn't have enough postage, they will return it for additional postage.

Call the cleverly-named Postal Answer Line to hear information about rates and information on less nebulous services—find the number in the phone book.

And remember: dogs can delay your mail! Keep an eye on yours.

BY MODEM

E-mail beats the USPS every time for its speed and low price, and of course it's easy easy easy. Add e-mail addresses to your mailing list and you can quickly send reminders to a bunch of mailboxes at once. No computer? People who have computers love to use them, so find a nerd to help with the dissemination.

Create Catchy Artwork

Do not give this responsibility to any member of your band who calls herself a fine artist—no sensitivity, thanks. Only large, obnoxious letters and a single, wack image will catch the alternative music lover's saturated attention.

Keep the words to a minimum and hook potential fans with your clever name blazing across some arresting picture. Sex (bare booty), violence (gun-toting bare booty), and drag queens (in holiday garb) theme regularly, but you know what you like. Newsstands and libraries, rife with illustrations, photos, and logos, wait to be plundered in the name of rock 'n' roll. You needn't look far for poster fodder, or even concern yourself with the legality of plagiarism; any image is fair game as long as you do not make any money from its use (no problem there). If attendance at the show is not important, break tradition and choose something tasteful; but nothing grabs the attention like a healthy dose of something shocking.

No one with visual skills in the band? Ask someone else to do the work, like the kids you babysit for—or what about that girl at school whose drawings won all those awards? They'll be psyched!

Day Job Procedures

Big corporate offices provide lots of things you need, like envelopes, pens, and an occasional paycheck—unfortunately they expect sensible pumps. Cool jobs where you can show up late wearing sneakers often don't have sophisticated duplicating equipment, well-stocked supply closets, or phone lines on every desk. In either case, keep in mind that the boss wants to know that you will work for International Waste Refrigeration Corp. forever, even if the job is clearly the most degrading and shitty allowed by law. Kowtow and satisfy as long as you can stomach it. They get over on you, and you will get over on them.

1. Form a trusted alliance at work and tell only that person about your band.

2. Keep a lot of "artsy" postcards or clippings lying around, stuck to your bulletin board, whatever, so that when your supervisor finds a flyer for the next Suicide Medicine gig over by the copier or picks up the phone when your Neanderthal guitar player calls, she won't be unnecessarily alarmed.

3. Do not let anything impede your access to the phone, photo-copier, and postage meter. Volunteer for those kinds of tasks that will bring you closer to the machinery you need. Sneak, lie, hide, bribe if you have to. If long-distance calls are re-stricted, make them from the phone on the fax machine or the boss's desk.

    The Pitney Bowes rules! It's the post office away from the post office, and with a little fraudulent activity, it's free. If your office has a mailroom, the person working in there usually closely guards the postage meter. You know what you gotta do: "I'm going down to the vending machine, Louie, want a box of Junior Mints?" A little bonding and bribing. It shouldn't take much. Mailroomers—the classic lowest of the low in any of-fice—usually spring at the chance to bilk their oppressors.

    If there's no mailroom attendant then you're stylin'. First, find the key and turn it on. Change the date to the current date. Then, press the button that rezeros the thing and enter the postage. If you have a huge stack, turn on the automatic feeder and dump them in, to-be-posted side up. For packages, a lever on the side lets you print on licky tape. Practice with official mail first, so that you don't waste time.

4. Make xeroxes of bios or flyers or whatever in groups of 25. Go to and from the copier with a couple of manila folders under

your arm containing all the shit. "1992 Insurance Procedures" or "FedEx Receipts" is a good label. Anything that will escape the attention of the curious co-worker.

5. Take the odd lunch hour; leave a little later than the rest of the gang so that you can sit at the boss's desk, feet up, using her phone to book a show in Ithaca and drawing some obscene thing for the next flyer on her embossed stationery.

6. Expect to eventually be fired, but try to keep the job as long as it takes to qualify for unemployment.

BY CLANDESTINE MANEUVER

No method of self-promotion matches the thrill of postering. It really brings out the ferocious rock spirit. First, make a poster using the recipe.

FIG. 15

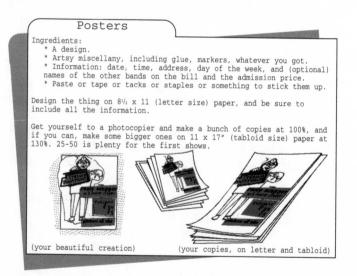

```
                    Posters
Ingredients:
    * A design.
    * Artsy miscellany, including glue, markers, whatever you got.
    * Information: date, time, address, day of the week, and (optional)
    names of the other bands on the bill and the admission price.
    * Paste or tape or tacks or staples or something to stick them up.

Design the thing on 8½ x 11 (letter size) paper, and be sure to
include all the information.

Get yourself to a photocopier and make a bunch of copies at 100%, and
if you can, make some bigger ones on 11 x 17" (tabloid size) paper at
130%. 25-50 is plenty for the first shows.
```

(your beautiful creation)   (your copies, on letter and tabloid)

A band member working at a copy shop or somewhere with photocopier access ensures that the posters will be printed up big, beautiful, and free of charge. Get one of these jobs and never worry about where your next poster will come from. (And, of course, menial labor motivates wonderfully.) However you get a date with the photocopier, make some copies on 11 × 17 paper and some on 8½ by 11 paper, to make small areas just as posterable as broad, empty walls. And get them printed on a lovely color to spice up those coffee-house bulletin boards.

Paste sticks the posters best because it adheres to nearly anything, but other methods are available. Staples (with a gun, not a stapler) are great if everything you poster onto is wood: unlikely. And you may not be able to play your instrument after clenching the staple gun all day. Could use tape, but its cons are many. It's noisy, and that's bad. You can't use it on any wet surface or anywhere really dirty or bumpy. Tape kind of sucks, in fact, unless you're indoors or putting posters on people's front doors. Bring a few thumb tacks—they're handy for bulletin boards. Generally, however, paste is best.

Approximately one pound of paste will hang about a hundred 11 × 17 posters. Although the package comes with instructions, the manufacturers didn't write them with your special needs in mind, so some interpretation will help. Look at Figure 16 on the following page.

Postering is nasty work. Smear paste on the selected surface, place the poster up there, and smear more paste and smooth the whole situation down until it sticks. Bits of city grub will splatter their way into your hair and clothes; as will bits of crumbling sides of brick buildings, dog-peed lightposts, human-peed doorways, rusted walls and gates. As the evening progresses, the paste goes from a wheaty, breakfast smell to a dirty-mud-barf smell. The muck gets on the brushes and into the bucket, and it will stick fast wherever you splash it on yourself. Prepare for some truly disgusting moments. Wear washable stuff and old, crappy boots—no suede—but make sure you look cute, because you may meet some new fans (guys who will love seeing you with a bucket in one hand and a picture of yourself in the other). They will come to the show.

Timing matters. If you hang your posters in a busy area any earlier

FIG. 16

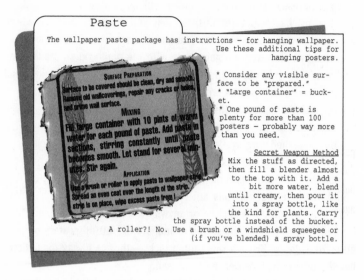

Paste

The wallpaper paste package has instructions — for hanging wallpaper.
Use these additional tips for
hanging posters.

SURFACE PREPARATION
Surface to be covered should be clean, dry and smooth.
Remove old wallcoverings, repair any cracks or holes,
and prime wall surface.

MIXING
Fill large container with 10 pints of warm
water for each pound of paste. Add paste in
sections, stirring constantly until paste
becomes smooth. Let stand for several minutes. Stir again.

APPLICATION
Use a brush or roller to apply paste to wallpaper strip.
Spread an even coat over the length of the strip.
strip is on place, wipe excess paste from

* Consider any visible surface to be "prepared."
* "Large container" = bucket.
* One pound of paste is
plenty for more than 100
posters — probably way more
than you need.

Secret Weapon Method
Mix the stuff as directed,
then fill a blender almost
to the top with it. Add a
bit more water, blend
until creamy, then pour it
into a spray bottle, like
the kind for plants. Carry
the spray bottle instead of the bucket.
A roller?! No. Use a brush or a windshield squeegee or
(if you've blended) a spray bottle.

than a week before the show, other bands will cover them up with their
own noise. Poster too late and not enough people will see them for a
Friday show. The best time to poster is Tuesday or Wednesday, unless
Monday is like President's Day or something and you expect the streets
to be full of potential fans. If the event is (unfortunately) scheduled for
Tuesday night, then poster Friday or Saturday and connect with some
weekend pedestrians. All this you do only at night when shop gates are
down, shop owners have gone home, and bored suburban kids with
money in their pockets (not little old ladies) stroll the streets.

Divvy up the adhesives and posters. Teams of two or more are best
in case of disaster or interference. Endo go with ecto, slacker with
workaholic, so half the team wears a friendly face for the outside world
and the other half plays the grouchy, whip-cracking role. Because the
square footage of effective, visible wall space is limited and the number
of neighborhood bands ain't, your posters may have to cover the hand-
iwork of others. Some would see this as a moral challenge: respecting
fellow artists while foisting your band to the forefront. You work it out.

In the meantime, choose the band whose show is the same night as yours or a band whose members you don't like, and target their posters. Leave not a one exposed.

*P*ostering in New York City

I don't know how it works in your town, but in my town, the New York City Health and Sanitation Code says you may not run around gluing and taping little things to public property. Sure, everyone does it, and the buildings, mailboxes, lampposts, and doorways of the East Village are plastered with notices about past and future Speedball Baby shows, but beware! Fines start at $50 for each offense; that is, each lamppost, mailbox, etc. A busy night of promotion could cost the band hundreds of dollars.

Usually, cops or sanitation officers who apprehend posterers committing their evil deeds will make them dump out the paste and toss the posters in the garbage, but they can also give summonses to anyone whose name appears on the poster— anyone in any of the bands listed, and especially the club. The club could be fined even if law enforcers do not catch any posterers. (I mean, duh, you glued the evidence all over town, they wouldn't have to work that hard.) Therefore, while breaking the law will probably enhance your naughty reputation, getting the club into trouble is a very bad idea, especially if it costs them money. Ask the booker what's cool and what's not before you start your criminal career. If you're really worried about getting the wrong reputation (you rebel!), call the cops or the sanitation department and ask what's OK in your neighborhood.

Hang your posters in heavily trafficked areas of hip neighborhoods, like near college art departments, coffeehouses, cool restaurants, used bookstores, the bike shop, the skate shop, the comic book store, etc. Don't bother blanketing the whole town, just go where you know people hang out who would like your music. Target nightclubs where other bands as cool as yours are appearing soon, especially if a big show is coming to town, so that all the kids at the Laughen Bones show on Thursday know to come to your show on Saturday.

Tour the neighborhood the next day (on your way to work your shift at the copy shop), and note which bands have covered your posters with theirs (probably before the paste was even dry) and which shop owners pulled the posters off their walls. Vow to dis them when you're huge.

BY MARKETING

*D*oes your newspaper have some kind of "What's Happening Around Town" section? How do you think the paper's editors decide to list the events that they do—the Quilt Fair, the outdoor Rachmaninoff concert, the free tour of the local fish farm? People working on the fair, the concert, and the farm asked them to, that's how. What's stopping you? Make a list of newspapers, magazines, fanzines, bulletin boards and radio stations in your area that you would look to for information about what's going on. Add the phone number, fax number, and address to the list. Then take a close look at the things on your list.

Get a recent issue of the publication or listen to the radio station and figure out how your band would fit in. For example, the radio station might have a specific show dedicated to local music, and the school paper always has a "What You Kids Are Up To" section. Local papers have a calendar of events. Call them up. Don't be shy, now, they probably have kids just like you running the place. Get yourself into a professional mood and here's what you say:

"*H*i, um, I'm in a band called Mr. Snuffluppagrass and we're playing a gig next Wednesday at the bandshell in the park. I was wondering if you could list the show in your Digable Concerts section of the paper. The Marbleville Teen Center is sponsoring the show." (Make sure you throw in any important facts that make the show more interesting.)

110

"Next Wednesday? We have a two-week lead time, so it's too late to list it in this edition."

"Oh, OK, well is there a writer who might be interested in reviewing the show? I can put her on the guest list."

If you can't stomach that conversation, just ask how far in advance the publication needs to receive information about an event in order to list it, then get the name of the person who compiles these listings and send her an invitation. Put all these people on your mailing list.

The booker may be able to help you with stuff like this, especially if the show takes place at a college or high school with its own radio station or newspaper.

BY CHANCE

The last and least reliable method of attracting a crowd is leaving it up to the club. If you're lucky enough to be playing at a club that buys ad space in the music section of a local paper, ask your booker to list your band in their ad—in big letters, please! Usually they just do this automatically, but one never knows. Tell her what you've done to attract people to the show, and she will be very pleased if you say you've sent invitations or hung posters around town. Knowing that you've worked seriously to draw a crowd may be important when she passes out the nickels at the end of the evening.

EFFORTLESS HYPE

The last method for promoting your band is not to promote your band at all. Looking out onto a room full of people when you get up on stage feels very good, and knowing that they stand there ready to experience your genius works better than any antidepressant on the market, but you kind of do have a responsibility to entertain these people—and they may have expectations!

Avoid it all. People will learn about your band without any special promotion at all, when other people talk about you; and good gossip is the most highly credible and important endorsement you'll ever achieve. You have plenty of time to let your following build up in your neighborhood based on word of mouth. An audience of real fans, not just people who loved your posters, will grow as your band becomes better and better. Yeah, I know you have a bunch of cool invitation ideas already, but writing great songs and putting on a tremendous show is always more important.

7

MUST HAVE CHOPS

(Human Resources Management)

NECESSARY MATERIALS: Endless patience and a strong stomach.

ATTITUDE: Styled to seduce or braced for the worst. Either way, keep empathy and etiquette at the fore.

FILTH FACTOR: Very high; watch for dirt-dishing and mud-slinging.

DANGEROUSNESS: Reasonably low, with the proper court-appointed restraining orders. (No, no, I'm kidding!)

OPPORTUNITIES FOR ROMANCE: Do you like surprises?

MUSICAL IMPORTANCE: So-so.

PRICE: Minimal.

TIME: Months, perhaps.

POTENTIAL FOR HUMILIATION: Mind your manners and keep it low.

h i n g s   c h a n g e , right? I don't need to give you that speech. You guys will probably get to a point where you want to improve the sound or the personality of the band, and it isn't going to happen with new equipment—it's going to happen with new people. As you all learn to play together and start crafting a unique sound, the lineup might change; new members come, old members go, players switch roles. If these changes improve the band, they make your substantial effort worthwhile, but if they weaken your relationships or upset everyone or even make you uncomfortable, then you have some hard decisions to make.

The types of situations described in this chapter, more than any others, force you to talk together about each other's skills and short-comings, to evaluate the band as a bunch of complicated relationships, and to become closer to everyone in the band. The things you do as a member of a group and words you choose will affect people's feelings; and you will face plenty of opportunities to release your inner sadist or measure your tolerance for abuse: asking someone to leave the band, adding a member to the band, quitting the band or begging someone not to go.

To keep the band's good karma intact you treat each other with respect and operate a loving establishment. To maintain your own sanity you must be totally honest with yourself when you face making tough decisions on your own. Many of these decisions will be based upon nothing but your feelings about the people you play music with, and sometimes it may seem like you have no way of knowing what's the right thing to do.

See what I'm getting at? It can be hard to leave something you've worked hard to make great, and just as hard to bring someone new into your project, but personnel shifts will often improve the band. They will make you a better musician by giving you chances to play with different people, to hear new musical ideas, to work on your skills, and to have fun with different sets of songs.

First, come to a conclusion about what the band needs and why. If you want someone to leave, know your reasons. Is it because you cannot stand them anymore, or because they come up with ideas that don't work musically, or because they never come to rehearsal on time? What's the problem? If you want someone new in the band, figure out what attributes you want for the band. Do you feel your sound needs another instrument or another voice? Is someone not able to pull their weight? Maybe you just like this extra person and want her around? What is it? When you honestly think about all these questions you can narrow down your search and come up with the best solution to your problem.

After you figure all this out, think about how you'll exact your changes. Basically, personnel movement falls into two categories: people come, people go. Let's start with the ones who come, because they don't trouble the psyche as much as the ones who go.

WORD O' MOUTH

Once you've decided exactly who you want, you can present the situation to potentials. Start asking around. As usual, word of mouth is your best tool, and other musicians can always help out. If everyone knows you need a new bandmate, then the perfect person will undoubtedly be among the people you meet and audition, and you couldn't possibly choose someone new who wasn't quite right. Spread the word in any way you can think and consider as many candidates as you can come up with, that way you have the most choices.

WANTED

Word of mouth should produce some immediate results, but when you've told everyone and haven't found the right person, hit the papers with a clever want ad. Kind of like "help wanted," kind of like the personals, music listings have their own particular language and format that communicate as much as possible in the smallest amount of space, because classified ads are sold by the line. Look at other ads and then write one that describes your dream date as accurately as possible—*without* excluding a huge swath of the eligible music-making population.

Anatomy of the Must Have
Chops Classified Ad

FIG. 17

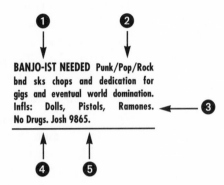

1) Classifieds are listed alphabetically, so begin yours with the most obvious information to get the attention of the banjo players out there as they scan the other banjo player ads.

2) Yes, of course your wholly unique music eludes *all categorization*. Categorize it anyway. Give readers at least a vague idea of what you sound like, so that you won't have to deal with banjo players who just want to play Phish covers.

3) Perhaps your inexperienced and unreviewed-by-the-press band lacks a specific sound. Use other bands as references *(Stereolab meets Sebadoh)*; or just list the bands you like—influences *(Infls: Ride, MBV, Boo Radleys)*. Curb the pretentious impulses when writing this part of the ad; you don't want to miss the chance to work with great musicians just because you're into a bunch of obscure bands no one's ever heard of *(Melodic Alt ala Swell Maps)*.

4) Special messages state your particular eccentricities *(No Hobbyists)*, goals for the band *(Ready To Gig)*, or fashion preferences *(No Grunge)*, and give the ad some personality.

5) Give the phone number of the person with fewest phone obstacles: not the

117

guitarist with three little sisters, not the banjo player with four lazy roommates, not the dead-beat singer who doesn't pay his phone bill.

Some other things to think about when writing the ad:

Obviously you don't let your English in-structor see how you irreverently throw spelling and grammar to the wind, but misspell another band's name and you will look really stupid.

Include any special accomplishments or at-tributes that will attract better musicians. You might not have a recording contract like these guys, but what about a rehearsal space, a van, a following of dedicated dormmates?!

Usually the band leaves their name out of the formula because current band members want to change the band's direction; because they don't want people who have heard their music to let their current image prevent them from auditioning; because they're replacing someone who is still in the band; or because they don't have a name yet.

Hello? Use abbreviations to cram more in-formation into less space, not to confuse readers.

GO TO THE SOURCE

Just like promoting a show, some well-placed posters and e-mail ac-tion may reach people that the grapevine

FIG. 18. RIP-OFF FLYER

misses. Use your newly developed promotional skills from Chapter 6 to advertise with flyers sporting those little rip-off sections that have phone numbers attached. Then ask at all the usual places: the music shop, record store, laundromat, etc.

If the personnel you want doesn't travel in the local rock circles—a cello player, for example—you'll have to plan some creative recruitment. Cello players probably don't scan the No Big Hair section of their local papers each week, but they might check out the music school newspaper or the bulletin board at the thrift store. Go there, leave your mark!

PIRACY

*T*he best place to find good musicians, of course, is in other bands. A little poaching might solve the human resources problem if you're having trouble finding that special someone. Seduce her or him thus:

1) Go to a show and stand right up front.

2) Decide whether the performer has what you need: great chops, big hair, and kick-ass equipment.

3) Say these things after the set: *"Great show, you're an outstanding drummer. No, really, are you in any other bands? [Good musicians commonly moonlight.] Because my band is looking for a drummer—that's them huddled over there staring at us while I do all the talking. Would you like to come and jam with us sometime? Cool, give me your number."*

OTHER POTENTIAL BANDMATES

Certainly, musical skills rank foremost when considering a new member for like, an orchestra or something, but a person could bring any number of creative attributes to the mix that don't include toned technique. What do *you* need? Do you need to surround yourself with friends? Do you need only people who have that special look? Do you need to create different noises and play music that defies all the local conventions? Do you need visual spectacle? Why not recruit band members based on haircuts or their ability to shimmy atop your amp throughout the set? I think you can see the liabilities of this kind of vanity, but so? It's your band.

Once you get the attention of some potential bandmate, chat a little about your situation and describe what you're looking for. Be honest about everything except any bad feelings within the organization. For example, if your current banjo player has been fighting with the bass player about who should sing backup parts, leave that out of the story and talk about how the band needs another vocalist. Then ask all the logical questions:

How long have you been playing banjo?
Were you in any other bands?
What kind of stuff do you listen to?
What kind of a band do you want to be in?
Can you rehearse twice a week?
Do you have a car/van/job/banjo/amp?

All that stuff is important, but personality matters most, so if the person sounds nice, arrange to meet them; and if they sound unpleasant, insane, or obnoxious, arrange to meet them as well.

Ask your victim to attend rehearsal, where she can get the general idea, see where you rehearse, see what equipment everyone plays, and hear how you sound. At the meeting, play her your songs and any works in progress, ask her to join in and see what happens. You'll get

120

an idea right away whether you like her and whether you could make music with her. If she seems to like your music and seems to like you guys, hold your applause until she leaves, then decide all together if you want to ask her to play with you again or tell her thanks but no thanks. Take your time, see everyone you can, and don't feel pressured to decide right away if someone seems OK but not great. If you find yourself using a lot of your imagination to fit her into the band, then she's OK but not great. Give everyone who falls short of Absolutely Not another chance to play with you, because nerves often spoil their first-time performances.

Auditioning is tough. Remember when you were seven and you ate dinner over at your friend's house whose parents were strange? The mom said take off your shoes and the dad looked at you mean and they made you bow your head and say grace before you got to eat the Tater Tots? That's how it feels to audition for a band—like an outsider sitting down with a family to dinner. You guys in the band all know what's going on; you know each other and you know the music. This poor person has not a clue! She's worried about what you think about her, she wants to impress you and play or sing well, and she probably wants to like you—a rather stressful situation. Be nice and make the person feel comfortable.

She was weird? He was geeky? They were rude? Matters not. Make nice to all. Auditioning sucks because everyone gets rejected sooner or later, and some people feel like losers all the time, so call everyone on the phone right away, respect their feelings, let them know what you're thinking and hang on to their numbers because you will see these people around. Calling people to let them down is a sucky task, but you guys are jerks if you don't do it.

Remember these rules of niceness:

1. Return every phone call.

2. Return every tape unless she says to keep it.

3. Call everyone who you didn't choose, and tell them these things:
   We've chosen someone else to play banjo for us, but it was

nice meeting you. You play banjo really well (and harmonica too, etc.). You'd be a great contribution to a band, and if we hear of anyone looking for a banjo player, we'll give them your number. Bye!

Watch out for: those who seem fucked up or talk too much about drugs; those with skills that blow you away (they may get bored); those with a master plan for the band (unless you're in the market for a dictator); weirdos; and people who really suck worse than you.

QUITTERS

Separation hurts harder than any personnel addition. People out-grow the band, get bored or frustrated, change their ideas about life, and leave the band. Graduate school, relationships, work, and creative differences might pull a bandmate from you. Let them go; if the band is your thing and not someone else's, keep your friendship intact by supporting anyone's decision to leave.

A nice shaking of the hands and parting of the ways might not happen, though. Intense, difficult moments can cause quitting. This is different. It's drama, and although it certainly makes for some good diary entries, don't take your quitter to heart. When people get all worked up during a fight or something, they should have a chance to just sort of let everything rest and give the problem some thought.

Quitter: I don't need your attitude, you dick! I can't help it Chris made me stay late. Your boss makes you do stupid shit every day.

Other guy: Yeah, but it doesn't interfere with the band. You're more than an hour late. We're all just sitting here waiting.

Q: Oh, whose fault is that? I just told you, he MADE ME stay. I had to stay at work!!

O: And you couldn't call? He said stay late and don't use the phone? That's so stupid.

Q: Stupid? Fuck you! You guys don't understand at all. I don't need this shit, so just find yourselves another banjo player because I don't need it. I QUIT!

Ok, obviously someone's in a bad mood and needs to take a little break. Wait at least twelve hours before calling to make sure she didn't actually quit.

After many months of songwriting and live shows, you may begin to see true personalities emerging and feel that perhaps rifts or problems divide the band. Catfights, sulking, apathy, and irritability are normal. I mean, *really* normal. You all came together as friends and now you have to work toward something. You have to do things that are not fun. Someone has to drive, someone has to make phone calls, someone has to act in charge.

You will spend so much time with these people and encounter so many personal situations together that the relationship grows way beyond what you could call a friendship—this is family, marriage, a business, the chain gang. When things get bad, you might find yourself saying things to a band member that you'd never, ever say to a boyfriend or girlfriend; you might use that high-decibel form of communication that you reserve for your little sister; you might throw yourself on the ground and cry and kick and scream like you haven't done since age five.

When you hang out with someone and they occasionally put you down or laugh too loud or pop their gum, it's funny *most of the time*; but after five hours in a car on your way to some show or after three hours of rehearsal, you may find yourself on the other side of *most of the time,* going ballistic.

The band will work your nerves once in a while, and that's OK, but a lot of things that happen in bands (just like in families) are *not* OK. You know you have a serious problem when someone does something frightening or violent, when you spend hours after rehearsal complaining on the phone, when someone just plain doesn't show up for something, or when you begin to hate doing anything with the group. Figure out your problem, because some problems have solutions and some do not.

If everyone wants the same things from the band, then most of your problems will have solutions. Try to work things out first. You can reschedule rehearsals for job madness or you can get a loan from mom for emergencies. A person with faltering skills can benefit from a tutor or from working alone with someone else in the band—suggest it. A person with troubles at home may need some extra handholding or even help from a counselor of some kind if their troubles are really bad— offer to go with them. A person with an out-of-control mean streak or temper might just need an occasional reminder. Communicate with your band when you feel frustrated and let them help think all this stuff through.

Personality problems really don't have such easy solutions: you either accept your bandmate's annoying behavior and try to deal with it somehow, or you do not stay in the same band. For example, if someone in the band is always late, you can buy her a watch, you can call her and remind her to get going, you can yell and threaten, but ultimately you either accept her behavior or one of you leaves. You can't change 'em.

Drug and alcohol addiction is the only thing that you should not even try to put up with. True, many brilliant musicians have had their chemical dependencies, but drugs didn't make them geniuses, and often their habits killed them.

You're not in their band. Remember, drugs are another type of problem altogether that has nothing to do with music and nothing to do with friendship.

When acts of kindness and understanding fail, you have to decide whether the problems will hold the band back or ruin the fun. Then you gotta do something.

SHE'S OUT!

Before you reconfigure (bust up) the band, think seriously about your future. Nice people who play well and like the kinds of music you do don't come along every day, and losing a member might disable the band to the point that you won't be able to play out or even rehearse. A new member has to learn your music and make other adjustments.

This is really an awful and difficult thing to do once you've decided to do it. First, don't tell anyone outside of the band that this unpleasant thing is coming, because the gossip will hurt your victim's feelings and make the whole situation worse. You want to remain friends afterward, right? Second, don't lie. If you want Germaine to leave the band because you think he spends too much time with his girlfriend and because you don't like his guitar playing, you should say so. And if you hate to tell him those things and sincerely hope that you can still be friends, you gotta tell him all that, too.

If you have no shows booked and your little band has gone nowhere, ask the offending member to take a hike. But if Toe Jam Bam has taken your town by storm and you've got a bunch of shows lined up, rotating the personnel presents a few problems. First, make a definite decision: we want Ed to leave the band. Then, decide whether you can talk to Ed about it. Will he play the shows you have booked or will he get mad and just go? If you think Ed won't play those shows, you have to cancel them *or* not tell him until they're over. Moral dilemma, and you're on your own. Things can get ugly. No one wants to be told by their friends that they can't cut it musically, or to feel that the band has plotted against them; but of course, that's exactly what *has* happened, so don't make the situation worse with shady dealings.

Put yourself in Ed's shoes: how totally embarrassing to be ejected from the band. He might be OK about it and agree that it's for the best, or he might get really angry.

YOUR TURN

Maybe it's time for you to go. Playing music with other people should not make you worried and depressed; you shouldn't feel gross during rehearsal or leave with lots of bad feelings about the people you play with and what has happened. If you one day realize that everyone in the band is a jerk and they don't make the kind of music you want, if you feel like your ideas never become songs, if you change your mind about this band thing, or if you just don't like it anymore, remember that you do live in a free country. It's only a rock band, after all. The whole thing should be fun.

Think it over carefully and then tell everyone in the band that you've decided to quit and explain your reasons. Don't blame anybody and don't apologize, but tell the truth: Marisol and I aren't getting along, and I don't feel like being in Killer Bears is fun anymore, so um, I'm leaving. Settle any unresolved money issues, shake hands, and stay friends.

8

NOISE TO TAPE

(Recording Your Music)

NECESSARY MATERIALS: Recording devices, complete songs, all your instruments.

ATTITUDE: Patient, faithful, and pumped. How perfectly can you play your music and still get along with one another?

FILTH FACTOR: How dirty do you like? Too much neatness will ruin your vibe, but too much grunge and you'll never get anywhere.

DANGEROUSNESS: Reasonably low, but keep an eye on unscrupulous vendors.

OPPORTUNITIES FOR ROMANCE: Forget it—too much hard work to let your mind wander.

MUSICAL IMPORTANCE: Very high.

PRICE: Big bucks required. You'll need to get those car washes and bake sales going.

TIME: A couple of days for some projects.

POTENTIAL FOR HUMILIATION: Pretty low, but you might surprise yourself.

Won't it be *glamorous? You wear those big head-phones and play your guitar while sitting on a stool in some giant, wood-paneled room. Then after your perfect take you'll run out into the lounge for another round of pinball or Mortal Kombat. Yeah, well, life isn't always as Metallica depicts it in their videos. Until some evil, oppressive music corporation forks over a million bucks. For now, hold tight to your artistic credibility and enjoy that macaroni and cheese—you'll be cheaping it.*

This chapter is just as rife with technical blah blah as the one on instruments, but in this chapter you don't have to learn everything yourself or beg for attention from some geek behind the counter. You get to choose your own geek—I mean, technical expert. And you may need several of them. Even musicians who have graced the studio many times often only have a peripheral understanding of the mysteries of sound reproduction. This chapter will graduate you to that group of musicians who has a better-than-peripheral understanding (lacking only the experience).

As your band progresses and word gets around, you will have many opportunities to record your music, usually by people who (just like you) are learning. Someone with an assistant-level job at a recording studio, for example, might offer to record your music after-hours when the boss isn't around. Someone with newly purchased recording equipment might want to play with their toys. We're not talking about recording your album, your single, or even your demo. This is a trial. You get to see how a recording is made, you get to work closely with someone outside the band in a creative capacity, and when it's over you get to hear one of your songs on tape. This experimental recording will help you learn and prepare for the real thing, when you make a demo or a record. Think of this tape as a sort of snapshot that captures the band's skill and progression at that moment.

You will learn a lot about your music during the recording process and even more when you listen to a tape of your efforts. You'll craft the sound of your band by these recordings, and later on, if listening to them doesn't embarrass you too much, they'll remind you how far you've come. By the time you are ready to record something to be released, you probably will already have been in the studio a few times and made several recordings—each one better than the last.

Just as playing live differs from rehearsal, a session in the recording studio is a third, distinct experience that rounds out your band's skills and brings you to another level. In rehearsal you relax, take your time and experiment. On stage, you work to put on a good show and ignore your mistakes (or at least make a good excuse for them). In the recording studio you take the opposite of both these approaches. Time in the studio costs mucho, so you make a specific plan before you go in and pay attention to the clock while you work. And in the studio, unlike on stage, little imperfections haunt you.

Take every opportunity and accept every reasonable offer to record your music. Going into the studio is never a waste of time because you can always learn something, and you will always have another chance to go back, so don't stress that what you do permanently represents the band. A trip to the studio may seem scary or like it's a big deal, and in some ways it is, but spend some time there and you will learn to relax and create in that atmosphere. Once you get used to the studio situation, you'll feel comfortable enough to have fun and work at the same time.

Every recording has a different purpose. The first several times you record, your efforts probably won't see the inside of too many car stereos and Walkmans other than your own. Rehearsal tapes serve as an audio notebook, to remind you how a particular jam went or to show the band some idea that you came up with alone. Crude methodology: place some kind of recording device—use your My First Sony if you want—in the middle of the place and press RECORD. It'll sound like crap, but who cares as long as you understand what you've recorded. No one else will hear it.

All other types of recordings (those that you'll let anyone outside the band hear) require professional assistance and more sophisticated equipment, because each subsequent recording effort exposes more people to your music. You can't use the My First Sony if the band has any of the following elements: a drum kit, amplified guitars or bass, or more than one vocalist—that eliminates most of you, I think. Even though these recordings will still happen on the lowest of budgets, you'll spend more time and money to produce them.

A clear-sounding tape produced with some professionalism will convince a club booker that you can write and play songs. Bookers hear a lot of really bad tapes, so they forgive a certain lack of quality, and future tapes will improve.

FIG. 19

TYPE OF TAPE	WHO'LL HEAR IT	HOW SHOULD IT SOUND?	FORMAT	PRICE
practice	you & the band	sort of hear what's going on	cassette	$0
demo	club bookers	hear songs pretty clearly	cassette	cheap
real demo	professional folks	somewhat great	reel-to-reel tape or DAT	not free
single	the entire world (hopefully)	awesome	reel-to-reel tape or DAT	even more

FOUR-TRACK RECORDING

The four-track records onto a regular cassette tape, and allows playback of four different channels of music at the same time. Any of the four inputs brings music onto one of the tracks. (You can only record onto one track at a time with most four-tracks, but with a real board, you will record onto many tracks at once.) Sort of the next-most-sophisticated step in recording, four-track units are small enough to use at home or in the rehearsal space, simple enough for a beginner to master, and cheap enough that someone you know probably has one you can borrow. They're fun! You can mess around and record all kinds of wack junk, and you learn about multitrack recording in the process—it helps prepare you for the real studio. A four-track also helps you write songs by yourself, putting your ideas next to one another and listening to different possibilities. It's so tiny you can set it up in your room, do a little guitar part, then a vocal line with a bass idea, etc. The quality of a four-track recording doesn't match other multi-track studio recordings, but if you work carefully, you can make a tape that will get shows and even work as a demo for the time being.

Anybody can work a four-track alone, but you need instructions. Use the instruction manual that comes with it (write to the manufacturer if you can't find one) or find someone who has worked with a four-track before and get a lesson. The four-track has four inputs. Don't confuse the inputs with the tracks. You can record using any or all of these inputs, but the sounds will all come together on a single track. So let's say you're tracking some vocals. You set up microphones for everyone who will sing, each going into one of the inputs on the four-track, and when you press record, all the noises from these microphones will go onto one of the four tracks.

Generally, no matter how complex the recording, you record the rhythm tracks first, then do bass, guitars and other instruments, and vocals last—a heirarchy based on fixability. Drum tracks are the least fixable, so you do them first, and you do them until they sound perfect. Working at home with the four-track, though, the order doesn't matter very much; just concentrate on getting your idea to tape and experimenting with different sounds.

Working in the rehearsal space with the rest of the band, begin recording with the drums. Place as many microphones as you can get your hands on around the kit: one inside the kick drum, two overhead to catch the cymbals, one near the snare. Get clever with the gaffer's tape if you don't have boom mike stands. Listen to each individual input through the earphones and try to make sure that everything sounds balanced and that the needles all seem to be peaking in the same range. Now hit record and let the drummer go for a bit. Play it back and see how balanced it sounds. Adjust the position of the microphones or the trim on the channel to pick up the weak parts and make things louder or softer. Then record and listen again to make more adjustments. Getting a satisfactory drum sound may take some time—patience, dear. Real engineers spend the whole day miking the drums in the recording studio to get a nice, balanced sound, but you're not an engineer (yet).

FIG. 20. THE MAGICAL FOUR-TRACK RECORDING UNIT

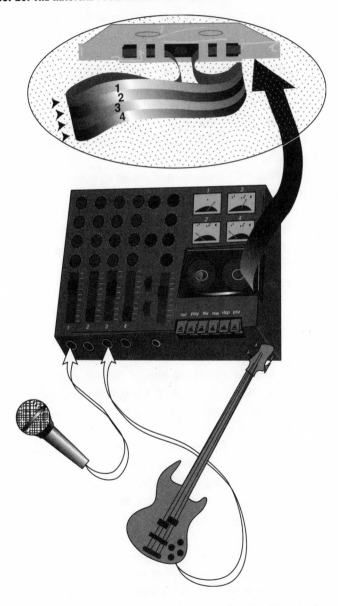

Plug your instruments or mikes into any of the thing's in-puts and record the noise onto one of four tracks on a regular cassette tape.

When you like the drum sounds you hear in the headphones, the drummer can record her track. If she gets confused playing the song alone and needs to hear the rest of the band, have them turn down their amp volumes or turn the amps away from the drums so that the mikes you've set up won't record guitar noises. Play the song as perfectly as possible, rewind and listen to see that it sounds good and that other instrument sounds aren't leaking in. If the drums sound lame and she can do a better take, record over the old one. You might have to play it many times until it sounds good to you.

After you finish the drums, rewind and set up to record track two—bass, guitar, vocals, whatever. For guitars, you can either mike the amp or simply plug the instrument into one of the inputs. Again, listen before you record to adjust the sound quality. Adjustments will be easier than with the drums because you only have to consider one input. The bass player or guitar player wears the headphones and lets the drum track guide her while she records her part. Play it back, like it, and record the other parts the same way.

What if four is not enough tracks? You can record more than one instrument onto a single track because you have four inputs to bring sounds to the track. You could theoretically record the bass and guitar and vocals on a single track, using three of the inputs. Recording the drums and bass on a single track is a pretty common compromise. Another solution is to record the first couple of tracks—drums, bass, rhythm guitar for example—and mix them down onto a fourth track, leaving three tracks free for a second guitar, keyboard, vocals, whatever. Once you get the hang of recording, you'll be able to do all these tricks.

When you've completed tracking the songs, you mix them down together onto a second tape using your tape deck. You can make certain parts louder or softer during the mix, fade the song out at the end, and eliminate entire tracks if you want. This mixed-down version becomes your master, which you'll make copies from. Keep the tape with all the tracks on it, so that you can rerecord or remix if you like.

In a few months you will outgrow this recording. The songs evolve, your playing improves, and the tape no longer represents your music.

Then you need to work in a professional studio and do a better recording that more accurately reflects your genius.

EIGHT- OR SIXTEEN- OR TWENTY-FOUR- TRACK RECORDING

More tracks allow you to record more music without having to put two different elements of the song onto a single track or mix things down onto one track. You definitely need the assistance of a skilled individual, however, because the multitrack deck is complicated.

You will preserve your recorded noises either by an old-school analog system or by the recent technology of a digital system. Both methods have their advantages and drawbacks, and just like the tube vs. solid-state amp controversy or the CD vs. vinyl argument, you'll encounter some sturdy attitudes about each method as you shop for a place to make your recording.

An analog system records voltages onto an open reel of magnetic tape, whose width determines the amount of information it can accurately store. Eight tracks go onto half-inch tape, twenty-four tracks go onto two-inch tape. As you record, microphones receive the sound waves and translate them into electric current. Cables whisk the current to the mixing board, where a producer messes with it, and then the tape deck head changes the current to magnetic flux and applies it to the tape. You won't hear *exactly* the noises you made when you play the tape back; but players and producers of rock music agree that recording onto tape brings a nice quality to the sound and that the tape itself adds its own nuances. Nearly all their records are made on analog tape.

But you are not making a record, and may not quite have the same budget for nuances as, say, Neil Young. A digital system can capture your lovely noises too, and will also lend its own distinct flavor to the sound quality. It works the same way as analog—sound wave, microphone, electric current, mixing board—up to that point. Then, a recorder makes a numerical sample of the wave forms, converts them to binary information, and stores them on DAT (digital audio tape), SVHS (similar to video tape), or even optical disc. Some people don't like it, but digital systems are convenient, small, and usually less expensive to buy and to use; this makes them more accessible to you. Someone you know may have a little studio in their house that will suit you perfectly.

FIND A STUDIO

Now you must find the proper setting to create your masterpieces, and the proper set of people to help you. Since you essentially hire these people—producer, engineer, and studio staff—and will work very closely with them to translate your musical ideas into sounds, you need to feel comfortable around them. Gossip now. Ask every person you can think of who has ever entered a recording studio to recommend someplace. Find out what they liked about it, what they hated, how much it cost, and get the dirt on the people they worked with. If a band went back to the same place twice, that's a pretty solid endorsement. Listen to the recording that they made at the place. Once you get some recommendations, call these studios and ask to hear their demo reel, a (cassette) tape with examples of work people did there. You may have to travel to make your recording. If the studios in your area are crappy, the mileage is worth it.

Tell the studio manager you want to make a demo and the number of songs you want to do. Many studios have demo package deals that include a list of services. Find out what they offer, what you will walk out with, and how much it costs. Make sure that your deal with the recording studio means you walk in with your equipment and your artistic genius and walk out with a finished product that you can take to a tape-dubbing place and say: "Please make a hundred of these."

These are the things you can expect to pay for:

1. Something to record the music on. A reel of two-inch tape costs over $100, depending on the length (as measured in minutes); a DAT costs about $35. Studios often have used reels of tape lying around that you can tape over, but they can't guarantee their quality. Whichever medium you record on, make sure that you have specifically purchased the master, because whoever owns the master owns the recording. This is not the same as owning the song or owning the copyright, and no one could reproduce and sell the recording without your consent, but the master's owner *could* refuse to let you do whatever you might want with the recording. (Worst case scenario: you record a cruddy, low-fi single and leave the tape at the recording studio because you can't pay the bill. Later, as a Democratic candidate for President, you want to release the single to show the world how hip you really are, and the studio says, "Sure you can use *our* tape, it will cost ya $100,000.") You record the song on your tape, it belongs to the band, and you will leave the studio with it.

2. Time in the studio. Usually based on per-hour or per-day rates. You guys who have never done it before will probably spend at least one eight-hour day to get three songs done, but the person who works with you should be able to estimate how long it will take, based on your tape and a discussion about the band's goals.

3. The attention of trained professionals. An engineer, a producer, and a mixer—usually the same person—will work with you in the studio. Bigger places might also have a studio manager who books your time and works out the money stuff; a technician who fixes and wrangles the equipment; and sometimes an assistant who, you know, assists.

Who Are These People?

If records were movies, directors would produce them, camera operators would engineer them, and editors would mix them; and they would *generally* divide the responsibilities like this.

Back in the old days, a **producer** would have a paternal sort of relationship with the band that would begin before they ever even went into the studio and might extend into all their future projects. The producer, who worked for the record company, would essentially join the band, contributing opinions about the music, the song structure, and the song arrangement. He (yes, it was always a he) would find the studio, hire the outside musicians, and organize the whole thing. He would also oversee the record in a conceptual way, helping make decisions about which songs to record, which songs to put on the record, and what the overall sound should be. He would "launch the act."

Some producers today still act as daddy, putting the whole project together and supervising its outcome, but just as many leave the details and decisions ultimately to the band. Even the most hands-off producer contributes creative ideas to every track on the record by applying his or her unique ear to the process. So technically, according to this vague definition, demos are too small-time to require a producer's before-during-and-after concentration, but we throw all these titles—producer, engineer, mixer—around loosely.

Engineers were traditionally science guys, with white lab coats and everything, who understood electrical manipulation. They, like, took physics. Today, engineering still requires attention to technical detail and knowledge of equipment to get the sounds onto the tape, get mixes off the tape, make sure all the gear works.

The **mixer** creates a final mix of the tracks. This happens after the recording session, and may happen on a different day, in a different studio. Mixer and producer may never cross paths. In the mix, different tracks are made more or less prominent (loud) according to how the song goes. For example, some parts of a guitar solo sound better louder, and some parts of it might sound best low and in the background. The person mixing the tracks controls that.

The roles of producer, engineer and mixer usually overlap, especially in a situation like yours: just a few songs, not much money to spend. Longer projects require more hands and more specialized technical work.

If the people you speak to on the phone are cool and the money seems at least sort of within your price range, go down with the whole band and check it out and have a real conversation with the studio manager. She will give you a tour of the place, describe some of the equipment, show you the rooms where recording takes place and rooms where mixing takes place. Notice the size of the room—could you all fit comfortably in there? Bring someone along who has experience in the recording studio who can offer a second opinion. Don't let the equipment overwhelm you, because the gear is secondary to the personality of the people and the place.

You may talk a little about money after you've seen the place. Studios generally set their rates by the hour, but they almost always offer a demo package that would bring the price down. If the grand total still frightens you, ask about off-hours or bumpability. Recording studios don't earn money unless someone books time. If Cindy Crawford has booked a month in a studio to work on the project that will launch her recording career, and she only plans to work Monday through Friday, that leaves the weekends free for the studio to book small projects—like yours—for less money. The studio may also offer you a discount if you allow them the option to bump you to another day or show up on short notice. They schedule your band for the weekend, with the understanding that if Cindy needs more time, they'll move you because she paid the big bucks. Either way, recording studios want you to make music, and they will almost always try to arrange something that you can afford.

I strongly recommend that negotiating a recording-session rate is the *only* type of wheeling and dealing you do. Some producers and some studios do spec (speculative) deals. They don't want any money unless something good happens to the band down the road. You could be asked to agree that when you make a record you will use these people, or that you'll give them a percentage of money you get in the future. Don't sign these kinds of agreements. It's better for everyone in the band to work a few extra weekends and come up with the cash now than to be obligated to do *anything* in the future. I mean, what if the producer turns out to suck? Or what if the studio just is not the greatest? It would mean that if you ever did get money, you couldn't go someplace better to record and you couldn't hire a producer who you really liked. You have more control over your music and more power in a situation when you don't owe anybody anything. Besides, nothing is free. You would still have to pay for the reel and for anyone's time who wasn't in on the deal.

Before you decide on a recording studio, find out who would engineer your recording and meet them if it's possible. The recording studio will usually set you up with someone who works there regularly, and knows their equipment well. This person will be more comfortable in that particular studio and won't waste any of your time struggling with unfamiliar equipment. You know how you want your music to sound, but only someone with technical expertise can achieve that sound, so you need the best relationship possible. Compare tastes in music. Find out what they have done, what bands they've worked with. If they could come see you play live, that is a great thing. Often sound people at clubs also do recording work, so you'll meet potential helpers as you play out. Bring CDs or tapes to the studio to illustrate sound things that are hard to describe; they make good references. Sound means more than words to a person who works all day with noises. Alas, cash will probably make your decision about where to record, but if you hate the engineer or if he doesn't seem to respect you or your music, those ten hours will seem like an eternity and the recording might not be as good as it could be—then you've wasted the money.

When you do decide on a place and an engineer, get all the specifics taken care of before you hand over the cash: Which days will you use the studio? What time will you start? Who will work with you? Will you use any of the studio's musical equipment (often they have tons of amps and drum stuff lying around that you can use in addition to your own instruments)? Does the engineer know what your lineup is and what you want to record? Will you be paying for the reel? When do they want to be paid? Can you use a credit card? Do they charge sales tax?

Make the most out of your time in the studio by preparing yourselves before you get there. First, decide which songs you want to record. Demos generally have three songs on them—enough for someone to get a good impression of your music. Record more, or record fewer, depending on your budget and whether you feel the songs are ready to be heard. It's important to know the songs you're going to do very well and to have played them together tons of times. The oldest songs in your set usually hang together tightest, and in the recording studio, small problems that you never paid attention to become very large, so go over these songs until you really know every part, because you will focus intensely on these parts in the studio.

The week before you're scheduled to go, make sure all your equipment works well. Play by yourself and listen for any extraneous noises: a loose pick guard that rattles, a squeaky foot pedal, an amp with background hum. You can't hear it when the whole band plays, but it will be there on the track and you will hear it on the recording.

Then rehearse your selected songs many times and discuss what, if anything, you would like to add to them. That's the magic of a recording—you can let your imagination go wild and add all the stuff you hear in your head: double the guitar parts for a bigger sound, double the vocals for a chorusy effect, sample an answering machine message from that wacky someone, whatever. These additional parts are called overdubs, and they are always really fun. If you want something on there that you don't know how to play, you should find a guest musician who will be able to come in for a short time and record it for you.

Here's what happens in the recording studio: You will separate different sounds of the song by recording each instrument or group of instruments on different parts of a tape. Once separated, you can control the way the parts will sound. You and the engineer work with each instrument to get the sound quality and the levels that you like, you record the tracks, then you mix them back together onto another tape. So, let's say you're recording with an eight-track board. You might record the bass on one track, vocals on two tracks, guitar on two tracks and drums on three tracks.

GETTING SOUNDS

After the engineer has her coffee, you'll start setting up and getting sounds, a similar process to sound check. Right now the room is probably empty, unless you're borrowing a house drum kit, and it will take several hours to set everything up and prepare to record. You record the sounds separately, even though the band plays all together, so you will all be in the room together. The engineer has to keep the sounds from leaking onto tracks where they don't belong. She contains the sound by putting amps in different rooms adjacent to the main room or by surrounding them with soundproof baffles. That way, when you listen to the guitar track, you only hear the guitar, not the whole band.

Drums first, as usual. The drums generally stay in the main room, so the band can all communicate visually while you play. Carefully placed microphones will pick up all their sounds (just like on stage): one goes inside the bass drum, one may go between the snare and hi-hat, and mikes dangling from booms pickup the cymbals and overall drum sound. The drummer sits and plays each part of the kit. The engineer may adjust the positions of the mikes, but mostly she's working at the board to get a beautiful, balanced sound.

When the drums sound good, the bass and guitars are next. As in a live situation, the bass often goes direct; but the engineer may also mike the amp. She mikes the guitar amps and you play, with your usual pedals, to get the noises you want.

Be prepared to set up in an unusual configuration, with amps in separate rooms or baffles in an awkward place. The engineer will get a sound from each instrument to play. It may sound different, but everything sounds a bit strange in the recording studio. Speak up if it sounds bad. Now, since you've separated all the sounds, you put on earphones to hear a mix of the whole band together that the engineer sends from the board. This mix is a reference that you'll use to hear instruments that are out of the room, or to hear less or more of certain instruments. The stuff you hear in the headphones doesn't sound like the sounds

FIG. 21. THE RECORDING STUDIO

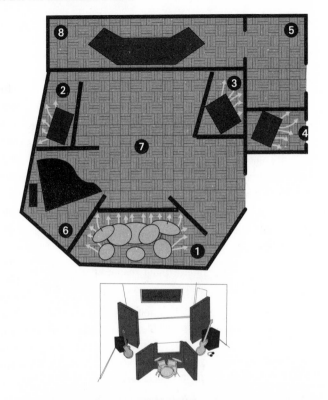

Recording studios are like theater stages; just big blank spaces waiting to be transformed by creative magic. Each one is different, but usually there's a big main room adjacent to the control room, with a smaller room or series of rooms off to the side, and a few windows in between. The room's skewed shape, wooden floor, and carpeted walls all prevent sounds from bouncing around uncontrolled and make every recording studio look like a mismeasured bachelor pad (brown, *always* brown). A good room lacks reverb and resonance and makes your instruments sound very nice.

The producer or engineer separates the instruments' sounds with baffles or by putting instruments (and sometimes personalities) in the different rooms. (1) The drummer always sets up in the main room, separated by windowed baffles so that the rest of the band can see and communicate. (2, 3) Amps face the wall, and baffles contain their sound. (4) Another amp in a separate room. (5) The singer might use this room. (6) A piano—there's always tons of gear lying around. (7) Guitar players stand here in the middle, wearing the big, clunky headphones. (8) In the control room, the producer has access to the mixing board and the tape.

that are being recorded and it doesn't sound like your finished tape will sound, so don't panic.

TRACKING

In this stage you'll do most of the recording. The vibe in the room has a big effect on your results during this part of the process, so relax, play the song, enjoy playing the song, and think about playing it well.

Often the first take goes really easily and sounds great, because the song is only happening for the first time that day. After that, you'll be thinking about what you did wrong or what's troubling you, and often subsequent takes are not as good, so warm up with a different song than the first one you want to record. Other things to think about:

- Pay attention to the time without rushing the process or getting nervous. Be ready to play when the engineer is ready for you.

- Do not distract the engineer when he's trying to listen to something, but do ask questions and learn as much as you can. If you get a lot of techie blah blah in response, ask for clarification. You are involved, this is your music, and you should understand as much of it as you want to understand.

- Be sure you like the sounds on the tape because, although you can fix some things later, your time will be limited then, too.

- Don't do drugs in the studio. Well, it's probably not a good idea. You're there to work. It might make you think the stuff sounds better than it does.

OVERDUBBING AND FIXING

Once you have the basic tracks recorded, you can fix small things and start doing overdubs. You can't fix or change the drum tracks (not on your budget anyway), so the drummer is done for the day unless she does percussion overdubs. You and the engineer will fix small mistakes on each particular track (there aren't any big mistakes, right?) by recording over them. Talk together about what needs to be fixed and whether it can be fixed. You will do these tracks by yourself, in the room with headphones to guide you. The engineer rolls the tape to the beginning of the offending part, you listen, and then start playing. He'll punch you in and out with precision.

Overdubs are the extra parts that you record after you track the basic stuff that you can't play live. Second guitar and vocal tracks are very common for backups or solos. Same as fixing a track, except that you will record an overdub on its own track.

Meanwhile the rest of the band hangs out in the control room laughing at the way the headphones look on you, or they sit in the other room watching TV. You may feel strange playing or singing that way, since you never do. At this point you've probably been working all day and you may be a little grumpy. Remain calm in the face of frustration and fuckup. Ask the engineer to help.

MIXING

The tracks you recorded provide the raw material for a polished, complete recording. The mixing happens in the control room, where your mixing professional will transfer all the tracks to another medium while varying their levels to achieve a pleasing sound.

Mixing is a pretty tough job. A row of levers called faders stretch across the mixing board, one for every track. The engineer knows what instrument occupies each track because he wrote it on a long piece of masking tape and stuck it there to remind him. Many of the tracks will not need any adjustment, but the guitar and vocal levels may fluctuate quite a bit during the song. As the tape plays, the mixer must push the faders up or down to accentuate parts of the song or correct mistakes. It's a complicated exercise in timing and memory. Fortunately, computers assist in the process at some recording studios. It works like this:

Mixer: OK, you guys, everyone get out of here. I'll make a rough mix and we'll see how it sounds.

(A half-hour later:)

Everyone in the band: Gee, it sounds great, Marc, but my tracks aren't loud enough!

Try to listen to the song as if you were hearing it for the first time. The mixer works to create a balance and find the right place for each instrument; she listens to the whole thing as she mixes it, but you the musician concentrate on your own part when you hear it. Listen carefully and speak your mind about the way it sounds, but at the same time, have a little faith in your engineer. Remember, she practically lives in the recording studio—it's only your first time.

Once you finish mixing the recording, you're pretty much done! The engineer will give you a DAT, and a few cassettes of the mix (depending on how late it is and how much you've all worked each other's nerves). Take the cassette home and listen to it with fresh ears after a couple of days just to make sure that everything sounds OK, and stay in touch with the studio to pick up your reel and pay your bill. Whoever takes the two-inch home should leave it in its box and store it someplace safe and dry and out of the way.

9

GRAFT, SHAFT, AND

HORROR

(The Music Industry)

NECESSARY MATERIALS: A band that appears to have some potential.

ATTITUDE: Indulge in a little paranoia.

FILTH FACTOR: Brace yourself for bullshit.

DANGEROUSNESS: Large sums of money may be involved; contracts and other legal things may change hands.

OPPORTUNITIES FOR ROMANCE: Far outweighed by opportunities for disillusionment.

MUSICAL IMPORTANCE: Some of the stuff in this chapter can detract from your music.

PRICE: You know better than to ask.

TIME: Not important.

POTENTIAL FOR HUMILIATION: Pretty low, since these are professional, not social situations.

147

Some of you enjoy organizin' and phone callin', especially if it might result in some good thing for the band. Others of you fear ugly words like business, money, contract, paperwork, and fax cover sheet. Most of you are already bored with this chapter. I'm sorry that the whole book can't be about having fun, but the economics are just too harsh—and besides, once people begin to pay attention to your band, they might approach you with business-related offers. You cannot avoid the financial bogies of making music if you want other people to hear it; and in case you haven't noticed, you've done a lot of business already.

A lot of your money, time, and effort goes into bettering your music, and bringing it to new ears. You deserve compensation and protection. Just because you are the "artist" and just because you like making music doesn't mean that you should never earn any money, but a lot of people in positions to take advantage of you assume that you will happily work for free. Club owners, for example, know that they can pay you last and pay you whatever they please because you probably won't argue; and if you do object to the conditions at the club, ten other bands are eagerly waiting to take your place. An entire part of the music industry will send their kids to Ivy League schools because of you, even if you never put out a record: music store owners, record store owners, rehearsal space owners, club owners, and other industry types.

By staying involved in the business stuff and paying attention to all the details, you can make the smartest decisions and maintain control over the band's future (and hopefully earn some of your money back). The business and legal stuff is actually pretty interesting once you get over the scariness, and you (yes, *you*) are capable of dealing with nearly all of it. When the time comes to begin a relationship with someone outside the band, someone like a manager or lawyer who will advise and steer you, you will understand a lot more about what they do and be able to take advantage of their experience, their skills and their resources.

This chapter is not about how to get a record deal. When your music is good (and perhaps even if it's bad), you will get a record deal. Instead, use the chapter to prepare yourself for the characters and situations that you will encounter if you keep going. You won't come up against them right away, some of them maybe not for years, but knowing the basics about the business will help you when you eventually need to protect your name, your songs, and yourselves against the tribulations of creative life.

First, take care of things that have already happened—dole out the dirty work. The one who hates to talk to new people on the phone can go to the post office instead. Discuss who will take on specific responsibilities—Marcy will book all the shows, Chris will take care of the van, etc.—so that everyone doesn't worry about everything. If you guys have your shit under control now, then when more serious issues come up you can handle them in stride. At the same time, look for sources of advice and knowledge outside of the band—sage words make decisions easier.

You can keep everything under control until the band actually prepares to sign a deal with a record label, and at that time you will probably need help and want to consider starting a professional relationship with someone outside the band. The relationship begins because you need help, not because you're too lazy to deal with the work of being in a band. "I hate doing the mailing list" is not a very solid reason to seek management. With a record deal pending, bands often start working with a team that includes someone from the record company, a lawyer to wrangle the contract, and a manager to oversee the whole project. Each of the three has a different point of view about the band, even though they all work for your ultimate success.

The Manager

Price for you: A band generally pays a manager as soon as the record company puts up some cash—20 percent, in most cases, of the band's earnings.

Ultimate goals: The manager's income and reputation depend on the band's success. She works for you.

The relationship: Of all these business types, the manager works closest with the band, doing bits and pieces of everything, buffering the artists from the icky day-to-day drudge while leaving them free to create. For example, if the label has given the band a budget to make a video, the manager will help find a director, set up a meeting for the band to discuss the concept, and fire the director if the band hates him, all while making sure not to go over budget.

The relationship between a manager and an artist is meant to be a lasting one—unlike others that end after a record or a tour is finished—so the manager becomes a part of the band, making plans for everyone's future.

A manager also maintains the band's professional relationships, including those with record label staff, attorney, producer, tour manager, everyone. These people often feel more comfortable having a third party to talk to so that the discussions remain calm and office-friendly. For example, a record label executive can complain to the manager about the band's music without worrying that they might bruise any delicate artistic temperament. And conversely, the manager will translate the band's succinct "fuck you, it's our music" into more professional language. The manager keeps everybody happy while representing the band's long-term best interest in legal discussions, financial arrangements and record company wranglings.

A good manager has a Rolodex of contacts and a reputation that makes others in the business eager to work with her again. And managers are heavy. They will fight battles for the band, give the band's reputation a boost, and use their experience to anticipate problems or strange situations. Managers rarely get paid until the band does, so they pick bands to work with based on how much faith they have in the music. This is good.

The Lawyer

Price for you: The lawyer, too, will get 15 to 20 percent of the money you earn when you get a deal.

Ultimate goals: The lawyer earns respect by fighting for the best deal for her client while maintaining neutrality in all other camps. Your deal determines her income, so she has a stake in your success. You have no obligation to continue working with a particular lawyer if things sour.

The relationship: We're not talking about a regular lawyer. Attorneys usually specialize in a certain kind of law, and the one you will be working with will be an entertainment lawyer, familiar with contracts, transactions, tricks of the music industry. Since the contract determines how the record company will treat you and your music, the people who make those contracts have the muscle you need.

Entertainment lawyers don't just represent artists. They represent producers, record companies, managers, and anyone else who may need a contract. Often, high-ranking record-industry types have the exact terms of their employment detailed in a contract with the label (to protect themselves when they're abruptly fired). So these few attorneys know everybody and have their hands in many aspects of the business.

Drawing up contracts only constitutes a portion of their work. Your attorney might drop your name at lunch with some bigwig; she might encourage influential people to come to your show; she might hook you up with a producer or tour manager or other important people—all in the interest of achieving the best record deal, and all with your blessing.

A&R Representative

A&R stands for Artists and Repertoire, a throwback term from the days when a record company told an artist what songs they would do and who would record them. For you, an A&R person acts as a liaison between the band and the record company—a tricky job. Read on.

Price for you: $0. The record company pays her.

Ultimate goals: An employee of the record company, the A&R rep works for your success but not necessarily toward your goals. For example, if you make a million dollars for Spinning Crud records, she will earn high-fives from her bosses. If you flop, she could lose her job. This means she won't necessarily be interested in seeing your band grow or change musically.

The relationship: A person in A&R is sort of a talent scout plus. She works to find bands that she thinks would do well if they were signed to the record label, and then she works with them once they sign a contract. Some record companies are small enough that this person has other responsibilities—like running the label—and others are so corporate that an entire department is needed to do the work.

She goes to clubs every night, reads fanzines, and talks to people about what bands are happening. If she likes a band—after seeing them play a bunch of times, meeting them, and starting a relationship—she makes an offer. If she signs the band, she then works to make sure that they fulfill their obligations, keep them happy, and help them whenever possible as they make their record. Depending on the size of the label and the amount of control they want to have over the band, the A&R person might go to recording sessions or even make decisions about the artwork.

All three of these characters want to see you succeed, but they have different ideas about what qualifies that success. The manager is the most on your side because of her long-term commitment, while the lawyer works for you from deal to deal, and the A&R rep has to work for the company—in theory. They share the ability to give you solid advice—even if the band isn't ready for a relationship—if you are sincere and ask nicely.

The best way to learn more about a professional relationship is to organize a meeting. If someone (a manager, lawyer or anyone) has approached the band about beginning a relationship, such a meeting should be pretty easy to set up. Once you sit down, ask how this person knows your band and what kind of relationship they envision.

If you want to get into the office of some lawyer or manager just to ask some questions, you'll face their demanding schedule of higher priorities and perhaps not-so-nice assistants. Remember this: anyone who genuinely loves music and works with young bands because they care that musicians get fair treatment will try to answer your questions. Don't be afraid to call the lawyer who represents your friend's band to ask about starting a relationship or even just to ask a question about some paperwork you have to do. If you feel intimidated by the secretary or whatever, write a polite letter explaining what you need help with.

Make it clear that you have no money and ask how bands without money arrange to compensate this person. When you begin a relationship with a lawyer or manager, they will receive part of your money if you ever make any.

Starting a team of people who will navigate the band to success is totally your decision, and you should carefully evaluate these people and the contributions they promise before you say yes to anything. Remember as you come in contact with the business fixtures that no one desires your success more than you do, no one will work as hard as you will, and no one is more dedicated to your music. But ask yourself:

- Do I feel comfortable with this person (you don't have to be best friends)?

- Could I call her with an emergency and get through? Is she too busy to deal with us?

- Does she seem professional and cool? Can I imagine her in some corporate meeting representing us and accurately relating the band's point of view?

- Does she have the corporate chops, the contacts and the big fat Rolodex?

- Did someone recommend her? How do the other bands she works with feel about her?

- Did she discuss a realistic plan for the band's success?

- What's the magic eight ball say? The tarot deck? In other words, go with your instincts.

Even though you let go of some of the responsibility in a professional relationship, you maintain control by communicating constantly and involving yourself in the plans. Take your time and make sure the decision feels right in your mind before making any personnel addition.

Each of the people joins the team because you choose them, so make the choice that you feel best about.

Other characters and companies will figure into your life in the even-more-distant future. In no particular order, I describe a few of them here.

BOOKING AGENT

Big or small agencies make tours their life. They know all the clubs and all the bookers. A booking agent puts you on the road and takes like 10 to 15 percent of the revenue you make.

RADIO PROMOTION

Radio stations don't just take a liking to certain records and decide to play them. No sir! How could they? Tons of records come out every week. Someone tells them what to play (or asks them nicely). Record companies want to make radio stations aware of certain records and to get airplay, so they have radio promotion departments or hire outside companies to "work the record to radio" with a kind of sales pitch, mail to the radio station, and follow-up phone calls. Even independent, small-time record labels spend significant cash on radio promotion, because when people hear something on the radio, they buy it.

MARKETING

Next, the label leans on the record stores with phone calls and niceties to get them to order more copies of the record and feature it prominently in the store. The label's own marketing department or an outside marketing company makes the store management aware of the band (especially if they're on tour or getting airplay); they arrange in-store appearances by the band, send a free copy of the record, whatever. In bigger stores and chains, the label pays to have the band's poster go up or even to have the record playing in the store or over the phone when a customer is on hold.

PUBLICITY

Record labels work with publicists, either on staff or within a public relations firm, to get the band noticed and featured by the media. Publicists maintain relationships with magazine writers and editors, newspaper reporters, TV producers, whatever. They come up with clever ideas and plan special events that bring attention to the band.

PUBLISHING

Music publishing is kind of complicated, but it constitutes revenue for the band. Basically, you are entitled to payment for public performances of your music: radio airplay, video broadcast, movies, TV commercials, even jukeboxes. Performing arts societies (ASCAP or BMI) will monitor and collect that money for you once you release something. Both have information for you to read, so write or call to learn more: ASCAP Membership Department, 1 Lincoln Plaza, New York, NY 10023, (212) 595–3050; BMI, 320 West 57th Street, New York, NY 10019, (212) 586–2000.

Next, some paperwork that will define your rights.

COPYRIGHT

A copyright protects your exclusive right to make and sell your artistic endeavors and to decide who can perform the music that you create. No one but you has these rights. The law protects you whether you do the paperwork or not, but the difference is in the punishment. By registering, you tell the world that you've protected your stuff and you can sue an infringer for statutory damages (amounts determined by the law) instead of just suing for the amount of lost revenue in the case of infringement on your non-registered work.

Registering is easy. The Copyright Office of the Library of Congress will happily send you their Form PA, the one for performing artists, when you call their copyright hotline, (202) 707-9100, or write for one to the Register of Copyrights, Library of Congress, Washington, D.C., 20559-6000. The fee is about $35, and you can register a bunch of songs at once.

TRADEMARK

A trademark protects your band's name, and you can apply for a trademark yourself, but there's a hitch. Go to the library, get the form and fill it out. However, if the trademark office turns up another band called Bingo Cadence Orchestra, you lose the $100 fee and you have to try again. A trademark search firm, separate from the government's office, will save you that sort of rejection by checking myriad sources (like the nation's phone books) for Bingo Cadence Orchestra, but it costs like $400 and then you still have to pay the not-cheap filing fee.

And the trademark registration guarantees nothing. Let's say you search, you pay, you register. Later you find a Bingo Cadence Orchestra alive and thriving in Butte, Montana. They've been around for 15 years playing polka and have released a bunch of records. The search missed them, but you lose because they first used the name and they can easily prove it. Using the name you've chosen protects you more solidly than anything else. If you have the money and really love your name, apply for a trademark to protect it. Otherwise, save any published mentions of the band or ads for shows with dates to show the judge later.

RECORDING CONTRACT

All recording contracts are different, and much too boring to include here, but they generally outline the following considerations:

- The number of albums (product commitment) that the band will do for the label.

- The amounts of money the band will get to make each album (advances), and the scale of royalties payments they will receive if any copies sell.

- How much creative control the band will have over the recording budget, hiring people to help make the records, artwork, and other creative decisions.

- When the record has to be finished (delivery requirement).

- When the record will come out (release commitment).

- What the deal is with using the band's music in films, on TV, in advertising, commercial tie-ins, compilations, samplers, etc.

- A budget for a tour, for advertising, for publicity, and promotion— if any.

Let these business relationships develop naturally. There's no need to go chasing down some manager just because it sounds cool to say, "I don't know, I'll ask my manager," or to drag some record company person to see your band before you're ready to play a really great show. Concentrate on making good music, writing good songs, and building a following of local people who come to your live shows. The rest will follow.

Your library, again, is a source for good information on the music business. Several good books out there go into all the detail that I don't here about record contracts, royalties, and musicians' rights. An in-depth book about the business is a good read for a musician who faces a more complicated situation, but also for anyone who thinks the music industry sounds like a fun career (and I won't make any cynical remarks at all about that).

At the Meeting

Got a meeting with a bigwig? First, determine what type of meeting it is.

At one type of meeting you will by wined and dined or at least lunched—lucky you. Someone wants something from you, so figure out what it is by asking many questions. Stay sober and be cool, as if you get wined and dined every day. Don't steal anything from the restaurant.

At another type of meeting you wine and dine your own self. You'll go to a lot of these with, like, a manager who is just starting her business or a booking agent who likes the band. No one wants to impress you, so just relax and chitchat and see what happens. Again, no theft.

You may go hungry at the third type of meeting, because you get together in someone's office to actually work—make some decisions and plan things together. You may be able to pilfer some free CDs to sell for lunch money, however. Bring a shopping bag.

Prepare yourself and the band by talking through any issues that are on the agenda, so that the band appears to have one opinion. Don't worry about how you look (you're an artist, remember), but you may want to bring a little notebook or scratch a few notes on a napkin. It's a very nerdy thing to do, but some of these people talk a lot, and afterward no one can remember exactly what anyone said or what conclusions were reached.

Keep in mind that a business person is in business to make money, which is necessarily distinct from your goal of making good music. Such a person is not your adversary, but he definitely sees things differently than the band does, and you may clash. Keep the band's goals at the top of your mind and be willing to work things out.

Act like a professional.

No fighting in front of anyone, and never gossip—it's tacky.

Once you make a record, you've crossed over into a different sort of territory. Suddenly the business stuff begins to make some sense because you think, "Hey, what if we actually sold a few of these? Shoot, why would anyone buy one—we gave them away to all of our friends." You may also develop a vague interest in selling records when you find that touring has inhibited your ability to earn money.

Those in the know call it moving units, and a lot of them don't care how you move them; whether you copy Nirvana or worship the Devil, it's all business. The basic unit-movement strategy over at the record company (regardless of its size) is to let people far and wide know about your band and your lovely release. Here's what they do:

Marketing gets your release onto record store shelves.
Promotion persuades radio stations to play it.
Tour support lets people outside of your little hamlet get a chance to hear you.
Publicity gets your names in some fanzines.

All these things work together and depend on one another. It does no good to be on the cover of *Spin* or to be on tour with some tremendously happening band if you have no record in the store for people to buy. And on the flipside, your sad little release will only gather dust on the record store shelves unless people have heard the band on the radio or seen a show or read about you; they need a reason to want to buy the thing.

Big ol' record companies have entire departments to take care of all this shit and push their bands. Why do you think it is that some band you've never heard of before is suddenly all over the radio, while ads for their record appear in every magazine and they tour through town with a band you *have* heard of? Because big record companies have piles of cash, duh.

Whether the company that releases your record is a filthy-rich corporation or a friendly indie, you and the band will still have to give their "pushing" some consideration.

By now you're probably covering your ears and choking back an honest reaction to all this unpleasant business talk. Even if you'd rather trim grandpa's toenails than read a book on the music industry, you should know what will happen to you once your band becomes a commodity. Your band's awareness that you will eventually need to protect your work and enter into a legal agreement to receive your hard-earned income is a good start. And besides, it won't diminish your level of artistry to know the difference between mechanical royalties and chewing gum—you can handle it.

THIS IS THE END

(Last Words of Advice and Disclaimer)

ell, my book has reached its end—good! You should not be sitting around reading books when you could be making noise and changing the face of pop music forever. I just hope you've found enough information and inspiration to get you started on your long and happy journey.

Remember that even though you just read an entire book on how to start a band, there aren't any rules. I urge you to proudly do things your way no matter what you face with your band; and I also strongly urge you to do it your way musically. You might never acquire the killer guitar chops, or learn to smoothly charm the club booker—so what? Not everyone can get to rehearsal on time or diligently practice every day—who cares? Those things are important, but music is much more important. Don't let the things you can't do stop you from creating; you can make interesting noises. Do something different and really enjoy yourself making music. Even though I have stressed throughout the book that there are really no rules you need to live by, I have actually compiled some, um, suggestions below.

- Don't get excited about free beer, get excited about free food.
  Drummer: No way, this is all for us?! Cool.
  Bass player: Forget about it, the opening band got a pizza.
  Drummer: Oh, dissed.

- Don't expect to put a single leaf of fresh food into your mouth on tour.
  Bored waitress: Yeah?
  Bored band: Moons Over My Hammy.

- Don't let your parents persuade you to study Communications or work at Staples when what you really want to do is filch off them and play drums all afternoon long.
  28 year-old slacker: But mom, I'm an artist!

- Don't ever call yourself an artist except when in some sort of discussion with a business person.
  Lead singer: Look, my job is to write the songs and play them on stage and look sexy. I can't worry about who's going to go pick up the T-shirts from the Tees Pleeze warehouse—I'm the artist.

- Don't let any journalists stay mad at you.
  Reviewer, typing: Why does this band exist? Perhaps to make sucky records.

- Don't expect to get laid right away.
  Attractive fan: Hey, want to come back to my place? My roommates are gone for the weekend.
  Lucky guitar player: Wow, you have a shower and a bathtub, right? I haven't had hot water for two weeks.
  Attractive fan: Uhh, that smell is coming from you?!

- Don't expect any money until after that.
  Evil promoter: Alright, girls here ya go, two hundred dollars.

Girl: But five thousand people came to see us tonight, Mr. Schmuck. Our van got a flat, our singer has the flu, and someone stole our guitars. Give us a break.

Evil promoter: I think I've been pretty generous already, ladies, what with all the free beer—but here's an extra ten dollars. See you next time.

• Say "hi" to me when you see me at Denny's.

GLOSSARY

Some of these words do not appear in the book, but you will eventually hear them. Learn now, impress your friends later.

Action *n.* The resistance offered by the guitar's strings when you press them to play. High action requires more pressure, and low action requires less. Only a technician can adjust the parts of the guitar that control its action—the nut, bridge, and neck—so pay attention to the action when you buy a guitar.

Advance *1. n.* Preparation for a show that involves the band's coordination with the club booker or promoter and the sound person. This work includes phone calls to confirm details of the booking, discuss

167

soundcheck, agree on a payment. (*See* Booking Agent.) 2. *n.* Money a band receives from the record company to make their album.

Bill *n.* A list of the bands scheduled to perform at a club on a particular night.

Board *n.* Mixing board, like at a recording studio or as part of a club's sound system.

Booker *n.* Person who decides which bands will play at a club, what time they will perform, when they will soundcheck, and how much money they will make. Usually clubs hire bookers full-time, but a booker may work for more than one venue.

Booking Agent *n.* Someone who sets up a tour for a band. The agent generally receives a percentage of what the band earns.

Capo *n.* A little clamp for the guitar fretboard that changes the guitar's tuning. When attached to the guitar, the capo stops all strings at a desired fret and raises their pitch.

Cardioid Microphone *n.* A microphone that takes in sound in a pattern similar to the way your eyes take in sights—from the front and sides but not from the back. This pattern of sensitivity corresponds to a geometric curve called a cardioid. It looks vaguely like a heart, thus the name.

FIG. 22. CARDIOID

Channel *n.* An input on a mixing board or multitrack recorder. (Don't confuse the channels with the tape's tracks.)

Chorus *1. n.* An effects pedal that splits the instrument's original output signal and makes it sound like several in unison. *2. n.* The part of a song that repeats its words and melody.

Coda *n.* "Tail," in Italian; the added-on, last part of a song or melody.

Compressor *n.* A device used in sound situations to keep the signal's amplitude within a certain range. Compression of a radio station's signal, for example, keeps all the noises you hear within a certain volume range so that a sudden musical burst won't blow your speakers. Compression on microphone inputs does the same for a live sound system.

Cutaway *adj.* A guitar shape that allows the player's fingers to reach the highest frets. A Gibson SG (*See* Figure 25, page 171), for example, features a double cutaway design.

FIG. 23. CUTAWAY

Dampen *v.* Muffle the sound. An old pillow inside the bass drum will dampen its sound.

DAT *n.* Digital Audio Tape (as opposed to analog); pronounced "dat."

Decibel *n.* (Abbreviated dB) A unit of measure used to logarithmically express loudness (ratios of change in power or signal levels). The "bel" part of the word comes from Alexander Graham Bell.

Delay *n.* An effect that repeats the sound, like an echo. Some really old delay units actually used tape, but today they do it digitally.

DI *n.* (Direct input; going direct) A technique for live sound and recording situations where an instrument's signal goes directly to a mixing board without traveling through an amp and microphone.

Direct Box *n.* A piece of equipment necessary for direct injection when playing live. The box takes the signal from the instrument and allows it to go both to an amp and to the mixing board. Direct boxes are used for the bass, acoustic guitars, and often keyboards.

Distortion *n.* The difference between the lovely smooth wave that an instrument produces and what you actually hear. In our world, distortion means the purposeful alteration that an instrument enjoys—from slight scratch to total breakup—when its sound travels through an amp or sound system. Achieve distortion by increasing the preamp signal or by using an effects pedal.

Draw *v.* Attract an audience.

Dynamic *1. n.* The relative loudness and softness within a piece of music. *2. adj.* Describes the song's energy, intensity, and its ability to get you moving.

Ebow *n.* Instead of plucking, you hold the battery-powered ebow over the guitar or bass string and its magnets cause the string to vibrate and sound like a violin bow might make it sound.

Equalization *n.* (Abbreviated *eq*) Eq allows you to change the quality of sound on a guitar, amp, mixing board, and even stereo by manipulating the signal's frequencies. The simplest example, a tone knob on a guitar, allows output of bassier frequencies when turned in one direction, treblier frequencies when turned the other way. A more complicated form of eq, the graphic equalizer, allows you to choose frequencies that fall between certain numerical ranges and either boost or lower them.

F-hole *n.* (Sound hole) Violins have them, so do other hollow- and semi-hollow–bodied instruments. They let the sound out as well as providing visual interest.

Fader *n.* Regulates the output level of each channel on the mixing board (twenty-four tracks, twenty-four faders). Push the faders up that control the guitar tracks, for example, and you'll hear more guitar. A standard feature of multitrack recording boards, but other types of mixing boards use faders, too.

Feedback *n.* A nice screech or howl that occurs in live situations when an amplified sound reenters a sound system through the same microphone or pickup that reproduced it, creating a loop. The guitarist controls feedback by positioning herself in relation to the amp. (*See* Figure 24.)

Flam *n.* A drum beat made by hitting one drum with both sticks at almost the same time.

Flanger *n.* An effects pedal that sends the one signal that it receives from the guitar out to the amp as two signals, in slightly different

FIG. 24. FEEDBACK

time, so that part of the sound hits the listener just before the rest of it.

Flying V *n.* A famous Gibson guitar whose name and shape are often copied.

FIG. 25

Famous Guitar Shapes: Fender Stratocaster, Gibson Flying V, Gibson SG, Fender Telecaster, Gibson Les Paul

Four-four *n.* The most basic and common time signature in pop music. Listen to a Ramones record.

Frequency *n.* The number of times a wave form cycles or repeats over a period of time, expressed by Hz.

Front-of-house *n.* (Abbreviated FOH) The mix created by a soundperson for the audience (as opposed to the mixes she creates for the band); also, the location of the main mixing position.

Fuzz *n.* Distortion.

Gain *n.* The amount of amplification in the preamp section of an amplifier.

Gate *n.* A device on a microphone that prevents it from recording unwanted sounds. The sound near the mike has to reach a certain level before the gate will open and allow the mike to receive it. A mike used to record snare drum sounds, for example, has a gate on it so that only the loud snare drum noises get through, and not background noises from the rest of the kit. Gates may also be used to activate certain effects, such as reverb.

Gauge *n.* String width.

Gig *n.* Dorky, archaic slang meaning a performance engagement for a musician.

Gobo *n.* A surface (usually clear Plexiglas) positioned to keep sound from bouncing all over the room. Originally developed for studio use, gobos are not uncommon in live sound.

Ground *v.* Your amp has enough electricity running through it to kill ya! But like all appliances, it's grounded to keep those electrons where they belong. You might get a little shock from the microphone as you touch the strings on the guitar, or from the guitar itself. The amp has a ground switch to change the electricity flow and by flipping the switch, you should eliminate the shocks. If not, have a professional check it out.

Harmonics *n.* In addition to the fundamental tone that a string produces—a G from the G string, for example—it also produces overtones, other frequencies that relate mathematically to the fundamental. Lightly touch the vibrating G string at its halfway point, the twelfth fret. You'll hear a harmonic.

Hertz *n.* A unit of measure of the frequency of vibration, such as those from a guitar string, speaker cone, or electrical signal. Equivalent to cycles per second, it is named for Heinrich Hertz and abbreviated "Hz."

Horn *n.* Part of a speaker used to control the direction of midrange frequencies.

Intonation *n.* The instrument's ability to stay in tune with itself. If the bridge lies straight, for example, and you have tuned the strings, any note played on any string will be in tune with the others. Poor intonation indicates that the guitar's bridge is wacky and needs repair. Intonation is a word you hear when buying a used instrument.

Kit *n.* Drum kit.

Leakage *n.* When a microphone picks up unintended noises. Guitars in a vocal mike, for example.

Les Paul *1. the man.* (Rhubarb Red) A musician and technician who began working with Gibson back in the early fifties to develop some of their most well-known guitars, including the Les Paul Junior, Les Paul Standard, and the SG. He also conceived some important multitrack recording methods. This amazing man still rocks today! *2. the guitar.* Gibson has been making Les Pauls since 1952. (*See* Figure 25, page 171)

Load in/out *n.* Bringing your equipment into or out of a club.

Microphone *n.* Converts sound vibrations into electrical impulses. Some mikes are more sensitive to certain frequency ranges and sound patterns, so that they work better for different instruments or for vocals.

Mix *1. n.* An arrangement of the tracks on a multitrack recording. Any set of separate tracks can be mixed in an infinite number of ways. *2. v.* To combine a series of recorded tracks by adjusting the levels of each track.

Monitor *n.* A speaker that sits on stage, facing the musicians. The sound person can create a different mix for the monitors than the audience hears.

Neck-through body *n.* The necks of some guitars are glued on, or bolted onto the body at its edge, but a neck-through goes inside and all the way to the bottom, and maintains greater stability.

One-off *n.* A deal with a record label for one record (the average deal usually provides for more).

Overdrive *v.* To cause the sound to distort by turning up the preamp gain or using an overdrive pedal.

Phase shift *n.* A slight time difference between two similar waveforms, which puts them out of phase with respect to each other, like the effect you'd hear if you took two recordings of the same sound and played them back, one just a fraction of a second faster than the other.

Pickup *n.* Electromechanical thingie that converts the vibrations of the guitar strings (or any acoustic instrument) into electrical impulses—like a microphone.

Plectrum *n.* Pick.

Preamp *1. n.* The section of an amplifier that prepares the incoming signal to be boosted to loud levels, with tone shaping and gain. *2. n.* A distortion pedal that simulates the effect of turning up the amp's preamp gain.

Presence *n.* A tone control on an amp, similar to treble, that gives the sound more of an edge.

Punch *v.* (Punch a guitar part in) A way of correcting small mistakes that have been recorded onto one of the tracks in the studio. The engineer cues up the tape and the musician plays the part correctly, recording over the offending part.

Reverb *n.* An effect that adds depth and a big-room kind of effect. Older tube amps often have a built-in reverb tank that passes the signal through springs of differing lengths. (Jiggle an amp with reverb and you'll hear this faraway-sounding crash as the springs bounce together.) Modern reverb units use digital techniques to get the effect.

Rig *n.* The pieces in an amp: head, cabinet, and any other toys the musician uses.

Seat *v.* To prepare a new drum head by putting it on the drum and tuning it.

Semi-hollow *n.* (Or semi-solid) A guitar or bass made partially from a solid piece of wood that also has a hollow portion to give the sound more resonance.

Send *n.* A noun, in this case. The cable going from mike to board, board to monitor or speaker.

Set *n.* The evening's repertoire.

Set List *n.* That piece of paper with the song order written on it that you swipe off the stage after your favorite band finishes.

Solid State *n.* (Transistor.) A type of electronic technology used in amps.

Spec *adj.* A situation where payment is contingent on future success. When the producer, for example, receives part of a record's profits instead of a fee for her services.

Standby *n.* An amp's tubes become fatigued when you turn them on and off, heating up and cooling down. A standby switch keeps the tube from totally cooling off, but turns the rest of the amp off.

Stratocaster *n.* Fender has been making this famous guitar since 1954. It was the first, and still one of the few, to have 3 pickups; and at the time, its skewed body shape seemed very modern. (See Figure 25, page 171)

Sunburst *n.* A particular guitar finish where the top of the guitar is darker at its edges, then fades to a brighter yellow.

Sustain *n.* The lingering tones of a note after it's played. Many amps have knobs that allow more or less sustain.

Tech *n.* A technically adept individual found in recording studios and in big-budget live sound situations. A tech takes care of equipment.

Tone controls *n.* A general term for any part of your equipment that alters the frequency balance of the signal, accenting either the lower end of the spectrum, the higher end, or the midrange. Amps, guitars, and mixing boards have tone controls, though they vary in sensitivity and variety, and usually have different names.

Top *n.* The front part of an acoustic guitar's body.

Trap *n.* (Contraption.) The drum kit.

Tremolo *1. n.* An effect that quickly wavers the volume of the signal, creating an echolike sound. Similar to vibrato. *2. n.* Tremolo bar (see *Whammy Bar*).

Tube *n.* Vacuum tube. Found inside amplifiers.

Two-inch *n.* A reel of professional tape used (primarily) in twenty-four track recording. It is (duh) two inches wide.

Vibrato *1. n.* An effect that varies the pitch slightly higher and lower than the fundamental signal. You hear opera singers do it during sustained notes. *2. n.* Vibrato tailpiece (see *Whammy Bar*).

Glossary

Wah Wah *n.* A pedal, often like the brake pedal on a car, that controls the tone. It goes from bass to treble.

Whammy Bar *n.* (Also called vibrato tailpiece, or tremolo bar) A removable lever that rotates the guitar's bridge, allowing the guitarist to bend notes. Pull and the strings move with the bridge to change the pitch. Often called tremolo units on Fender guitars; even though tremolo and vibrato are different effects, the basic mechanism is the same.

INDEX

Index

Index

Index

About the Author

Kathryn Lineberger graduated from City University of New York in 1994, and has written about music and fashion for such magazines as *Spin, Harper's Bazaar* and *In Fashion.* She plays bass in Fluffer, whose latest album is *Ask Me What It Feels Like,* on Link Records. Kathy escaped the dreary suburbs of Ohio for New York City as a teenager, and still lives there today. *The Rock Band Handbook* is her first book.